LEADING WITH KINDNESS

LEADING WITH KINDNESS

HOW GOOD PEOPLE CONSISTENTLY GET SUPERIOR RESULTS

William F. Baker, Ph.D.

Michael O'Malley, Ph.D.

HARPERCOLLINS
LEADERSHIP

AN IMPRINT OF HARPERCOLLINS

Leading with Kindness

Published by HarperCollins Leadership, an imprint of HarperCollins Focus LLC.

Bulk discounts available. For details visit:
www.harpercollinsleadership.com/bulkquotes
Email: customercare@harpercollins.com

ISBN 978-0-8144-3942-5

To the loves of our lives,
JEANNEMARIE and STEPHANIE

CONTENTS

In *Leading with Kindness: How Good People Consistently Get Superior Results*, Bill Baker and Michael O'Malley explore how one of the most unheralded features of leadership—basic human kindness—drives successful organizations. The authors' creativity, experience, and first-rate intellect have produced a book of original and relevant insights, resulting in a significant contribution to this most scrutinized of subjects.

While people generally recognize that a leader's emotional intelligence factors into that person's leadership style, most are reluctant to judge it as being as important as analytical ability, decision-making skills, or proficiency in execution. Such emotions as compassion, empathy, and kindness are often dismissed as unquantifiable in their impact on organizations or are mistaken for weakness. Yet, research in neuroscience and social sciences clearly reveals the physiological and cultural basis of emotional resonance in social networks and its measurable effects on both individual and group performance.

Great leaders have always relied on emotion to get things done: Managers inspire employees to collaborate, coaches rally players to win games, and politicians persuade voters to elect them. But kindness, the leadership emotion that Baker and O'Malley focus on, is not what people immediately associate with business, let alone with their boss. The "do-as-I-say," command-and-control leadership model of 20th-century business organizations or the Dickensian factory owner of much of the 19th-century linger in our collective consciousness.

Business scholars and practitioners alike, however, know that performance is maximized when people feel supported and are motivated through positive means—namely, kindness. Drawing on organizational theory, interviews with the sharpest minds in business, education, and the nonprofit sector, and more than half a century of experience in business and academia, the authors demonstrate why kindness is a core competency in the leadership skill set and how it drives productive behaviors of high-performing individuals and teams in today's best-run companies.

At Columbia Business School, our Program on Social Intelligence is a direct response to ever-changing business demands, and it addresses many of the same leadership dimensions that Baker and O'Malley examine. In the past, professionals typically devoted their entire careers to companies that valued their functional or technical skills, not their social ones. Today's lightning-fast business environment demands job candidates who can step into senior management roles in five to eight years, often in decentralized and constantly transforming enterprises, in relationship-based professions like investment banking and consulting, and in dynamic and diverse communities. In such organizations, leadership success is often defined in interpersonal terms: knowing how and when to collaborate or command, how to lead and develop subordinates, or how to manage and empower networks.

Excellent leaders are also "kind" to themselves by making their personal growth a career-long priority. Above all, they cultivate self-awareness. Their awareness helps them to appreciate their strengths and limitations, respect and empathize with others, stay open to new ideas, embrace differences, maintain control of their emotions during difficult times, and adapt positively to obstacles and opportunities.

Traditional models of leadership have favored the technical (quantitative) over the emotional (qualitative) dimension of leadership. Ironically, as technology grows geometrically more powerful and machines manage more of the analytics, our leaders must become more human, perhaps more humane. *Leading with Kindness: How Good People Consistently Get Superior Results* advocates a balance, just as we do in academia. To excel today, business leaders must master both quantitative skills such as finance, statistics, and accounting, and those less easily quantified, like communications, people development, and team-building.

As Baker and O'Malley rightly point out, the ability to leverage one's kindness is not a soft skill. On the contrary, it is a no-nonsense approach to business that can return hard dividends in organizational effectiveness and business performance. Most important, leaders can learn to behave with compassion. For the beginner, this book is a good first lesson. For the seasoned leader, it is a gentle and often entertaining reminder that there is no time like the present for mastering this essential and powerful human dimension.

Glenn Hubbard
Dean and Russell L. Carson
Professor of Finance and Economics
Columbia Business School
New York City
April 2008

This work was many years in the making, starting with ongoing discussions about leadership with my co-author, Michael O'Malley. We routinely compared notes and observations about both the nature and mechanics of successful leaders, and what made them distinct from the pretenders and also-rans. Then, in January 2004, much of what we had been talking about coalesced when two of my favorite subjects converged: the art of television and the business of management. Like the shot heard round the world, the simple words "You're fired!" were quoted everywhere; the man who imperiously used these words on his humbling, dog-eat-dog television reality series envisioned a trademarked empire with the phrase emblazoned on his own line of clothing, among other things.

What made Donald Trump's *The Apprentice* such a phenomenon? Why did more than 20 million viewers tune in every week to watch the axe fall decisively and mercilessly upon the latest entrepreneurial reject? Much of the credit can go directly to "The Donald," a celebrity CEO with a larger-than-life personality. But another major factor was undoubtedly the allure of power associated with people in high places. Having the authority to make important decisions, give directives, and delegate work to subordinates is an intoxicating prospect. Yet great responsibility comes with rank, and those who reach positions of authority will find the discharge of their duties to be more challenging than they imagined.

If you want to be good at managing, you had better be prepared for a lifetime of learning—learning before doing, learning by doing, and learning by failure—and introspection, observation, and trial and error. If you are fortunate, as I was, you will have a chance to, shall we say, apprentice under wise and generous counsel. Some of my earliest and most valuable lessons in management came from my father, a sweet and gentle man who was a skilled factory worker in Cleveland, Ohio. As a child, I saw that my father was both frustrated by the indifference of his supervisors and puzzled why a man who wanted to give his heart and mind to the job was asked only to use his hands. Nevertheless, his hard work and leadership abilities were eventually recognized, and he was promoted to foreman. Practicing a very different style of management from Mr. Trump, he was well liked and respected by all of the line workers. When I asked my father his secret to good management, he told me that he just tried to treat the men fairly and give the best advice he could about getting the job done and done right.

When I was a teenager, a psychologist moved in next door to our home. An *industrial* psychologist—exactly the right neighbor to nourish my growing interest in management. He had been a professor at Ohio State University and was happy to take me under his wing. He shared details of his consulting work with me and even let me observe his interviews. This was heady stuff for a seventeen-year-old. Little did I know that this was just the beginning of lifelong instruction in leadership. Case Western Reserve University, in my hometown of Cleveland, offered an excellent program in industrial psychology, so I took graduate courses while I worked in radio and television. I figured that the field of industrial psychology would be my backup plan, after the inevitable implosion of my burgeoning show business career.

Ultimately, I earned a Ph.D. in Communications and Organizational Behavior. Although I never formally put that education to work, the training served me well throughout my long career in broadcasting—not in front of the mike, but behind the scenes, managing stations and media companies. Despite the success I've had, the truth of the matter is that the idea of managing others always felt daunting to me. I never thought of managing as a job, as something you do, but more as an art, something you refine and perfect with time. Wanting to do well, combined with needing to do well for the sake of others, is a weighty obligation. After all, this art isn't practiced on canvas, but with real people with real homes and families.

Thankfully more help arrived. In addition to my dear father, with his unerring advice born of experience and common sense, another person has nurtured and shaped my skills as a manager. Jeannemarie, my wife of 39 years, is a psychiatric nurse practitioner and a former professor at Columbia University. She is a very compassionate and loving person who has touched countless lives in her work as a family therapist and as a friend in her personal relationships. Over the years, I have had occasion to learn about family systems from Jeannemarie. As applied to the workplace—which can resemble extended, sometimes dysfunctional, families—the theory of family systems maintains that employees tend to replicate the roles they played in their families of origin. This very Freudian thought simply suggests that we acquire values and develop customary ways of relating to others based on our experiences with family and friends.

The ideas behind family systems are helpful, if for no other reason than to highlight the fact that when people enter organizations, they are not suddenly cut off from their emotional lives. We may expect people to behave in a certain way in business settings, but people come bundled with attitudes, aspirations, and needs, which are expressed in a variety of ways, depending on the nature and quality of relations that are forged in organizations. Therefore, employees will respond in various ways to different styles of leadership.

Media businesses are particularly interesting and complex because of the big egos that fill hallways like puffer fish and the surprising insecurities among the on-air talent. If you want to practice systems theory under the most trying circumstances, then have a go at practicing in the entertainment industry! You won't find a more complex web of relationships or more diverse set of personalities. I have had valuable opportunities to fine-tune my management style over the years, both as president for a decade of Westinghouse Television and as the 20-year president of the flagship public broadcasting station WNET in New York City and as a member of several boards—mainly in the for-profit and nonprofit arts and entertainment worlds.

I am still deciphering the nuances of human nature, trying to discover the most effective ways to lead and motivate people. I have tried to make use of the theories I've been taught, the books I've read, and the lessons I've learned. Among some of the best advice and information I have received and collected, a common thread is that successful management doesn't have to be in the style of Donald Trump, at least not as demonstrated on his popular show.

Together with my friend, psychologist and fellow Clevelander, Mike O'Malley, I decided to write this book in order to advocate a different kind of management—a more progressive one based on an understanding of the individual and an appreciation of the unique talents and contributions each person can offer.

Bill Baker
New York City, 2008

················ A C K N O W L E D G M E N T S ···············

We are indebted to the many executives who graciously contributed their ideas to this work, who commented on earlier
versions, and who, as they have done for so many others, inspired
us. Ultimately, however, we are solely responsible for the contents
of this book. We also appreciate the hard work put in by the team
at AMACOM and are especially grateful to Christina Parisi and
Jim Bessent for their editorial expertise. Finally, we wish to thank
Jennifer Hassan and Susan Neitlich for their incisive remarks and
suggestions as the manuscript developed.

T his work was born of a need to let others know that, contrary to scintillating news reports of corporate bad behavior, the business world is populated by many fine men and women. Your family, friends, and neighbors have responsible positions in organizations of different shapes and sizes. They are people who deeply care about future generations, the communities in which they live, and the myriad social causes that can raise the standard of living and quality of life in America. They are brothers and sisters, sons and daughters, fathers and mothers who are earth-bound Joes and Janes with the same concerns and wishes as anyone else: to live well and to make a difference.

The leaders we have in mind don't seek out the spotlight or advertise their good deeds. They don't bask in virtuousness or revel in their achievements. They don't entertain themselves with their wealth or use their rank to distance themselves from the rest of humanity. They muddle through life much like the rest of us, mostly unnoticed except by those around them who are keenly aware that they are in the presence of someone special.

These inconspicuous leaders weren't always the norm. Once upon a time, but not too far away or long ago, many leaders had the tact of bulldozers and dwelled in exclusionary executive nests that were sealed more tightly than mermaids' purses. They believed they had both the power and the right to push people around. As recently as the 1980s, Robert Nuslott, the CEO of the Chicago-based manufacturer FMC, was quoted as saying: "Leadership is demonstrated when the ability to inflict pain is confirmed."[1] Lest we think of two decades as bygone years, there have been plenty of examples in the intermediate years between then and now of leaders who run roughshod over we puny mortals—and to whom many observers bestowed much adulation: think Chainsaw Al and others of his ilk.

That old-style flagellation doesn't work any more—not that it ever was a formidable contender for enlightened management. But more employees were willing to tolerate the pain as part of a bargain they struck with the Devil. In exchange for high wages, lucrative benefits, and job security, employees were willing to endure a sizable allotment of disparagement while hoping for better in their spare time. As the economy and workforce changed, however, that tacit agreement rapidly unwound.

The emergence of new economic powerhouses and competitors around the globe has eaten away at privileged American monopolies in certain industrial sectors, with a subsequent erosion of worker pay and benefits and the draconian loss of jobs. Simultaneously, the knowledge workers who Peter Drucker predicted would appear on the scene, did.[2] Unlike the traditional employer-employee association of yore, these employees carried the tools of their trades in their heads. Less dependent on specific companies for their material nourishment, they operated more like a Silicon Valley caliphate: nomadic technologists who roamed from company to company in search of a better deal and more exciting work. What's more, there wasn't a limitless supply of these people, and there were important individual differences—particular individuals were more sought after than others. More and more, companies found themselves dependent on a scarce, variable pool of human resources.

There is no firm contract with knowledge workers. They come and they go. Now, however, when too many go, all eyes turn toward the manager who couldn't keep them—who allowed rare talent to walk out the door and incurred the expense of hiring replacements. When the talent flees in droves, now, more often than not, bad management is blamed. We can assure you that the variety of management responsible for mass employee defections isn't adhering to the kindly leadership we will be discussing throughout this book.

The founder of Wikipedia, Jimmy "Jimbo" Wales, has it right when he says that the way to manage in today's environment is to treat workers as volunteers—you can't just tell them what to do. When the right people are deployed in the right ways, a lot of directives aren't necessary.[3] In the case of Wikipedia, managing volunteers was literally true, but Wales's comments were intended to apply more broadly to the modern company. It is a wholesome outlook. We appreciate volunteers and understand that they are there with you by choice. The idea of employee-as-volunteer forces leaders to give much greater thought to what employees hope to derive from the employee-employer relationship and what elements of the job and work environment will keep them engaged. Suddenly, employees matter; and the way leaders interact with them matters, too. Some companies, such as Best Buy, are experimenting with the extreme freedom advocated by organizational commentators like Wales, with positive effects. By redefining work as something people *do* versus where they are, how long they work, or the number of activities in which they are engaged, Best Buy has been changing its culture to one that emphasizes productivity regardless of when or where the work is undertaken—to the point at which even meetings are optional. That is, the company hopes to replace busyness with effectiveness. Early results are promising: Productivity is up 35 percent where the program has been implemented, and turnover is down more than 50 percent (*American Morning*, CNN, January 14, 2008).

This book is our opportunity to discuss leadership as it always ought to have been practiced, a form of leadership that assumes more importance than ever in a volatile business climate in which a premium is placed on those who can lead well. We entered this project with ideas about what constitutes superior leadership based on a combined sixty-plus years in business and academia: enough time and experience to formulate an opinion. But from there we proceeded reflexively. That is, we put our ideas to the test, against both research results from the management literature and the quality leaders with whom we spoke about our leadership ideas. In some cases, we were forced to rethink and retest a position. Thus, although we started this book with a working structure, our concepts of kind leadership evolved as new evidence became available. We conscientiously tried to avoid Procrustean temptations to force-fit the extant facts into our preconceptions. Similarly, we did not blindly accept information we gathered as true unless it was corroborated by other findings or withstood the scrutiny of common sense.

The leaders we spoke with had varied backgrounds and business trajectories. Some started and built their own companies, and some took more established routes through the corporate hierarchy. Collectively, they had experience in both for-profit and not-for-profit organizations. They represented different industries, generations, and geographies. We learned immensely from each (brief biographies of each of our interviewees are located in the appendix).

Whereas each man and woman had the requisite values, traits, and abilities to qualify as a kind leader, during our discussions with them each emphasized slightly different aspects of leadership. Throughout the book we will selectively highlight their leadership philosophies and place them within the broader context of what it means to lead with kindness.

A recent conversation during a visit to a financial institution summed up the type of leaders we chose as our subjects. As conversation moved to the topic of this book, the president of the company asked us who we had spoken to. Given where we were, we started with leaders of financial companies: "Tom Renyi . . ." The president stopped us before we even made it to the second name. "Tom Renyi! He is the most honorable man in banking."

We don't use the word much elsewhere in this book, so now would be an opportune time to say that *honorable* gives a good description of those who contributed their ideas to this book. Honorable, because the sum total of who they are and what they achieved is worthy of esteem and respect. However, not one of these leaders would claim that he scaled organizational heights alone, or developed into the person he is without some assistance—sometimes hefty pushes—along the way. Thus, en route to our discussion of kindness, these people gave us what we refer to as *the first rule of success*. The rule needs to be satisfied before you can meaningfully move on to the many other principles of success, offered in sets of three, five, seven, or ten in the abundant self-help literature. The first rule of success is to find someone who can help you to succeed. *No one* achieves her life's ambitions without the steady, guiding hands of others.

In a way, this book begins at the end. In the appendix, we provide a description of leaders who already have benefited from the selfless giving of others and who are now in the process of giving back. They have been shaped by mentors who had nothing more to gain than to watch someone in whom they saw great potential develop and flourish.

Despite the well-documented, positive influences of mentors on careers,[4] not everyone is blessed with a mentor or adept at finding one.

The first and most powerful mentors in most people's lives—parents—aren't equally gifted, for an assortment of reasons. Interestingly, but not surprisingly, several leaders we interviewed mentioned that their parents had the most profound effects on their worldviews and professional successes, instilling values, such as tenacity, and skills, such as peacemaking (conflict resolution), that are useful anywhere, any time.

Second, although there are many willing and able potential mentors, it takes a keen and accepting eye to locate them and take advantage of what they have to offer. Mentors walk among us ghost-like, and only certain people are able to see them. The kind leaders we discuss throughout this book are open to experience and persistently look for ways to improve, and, consequently, are able to notice and receive what others are willing to give. They don't have the counterproductive sensibilities that prevent many people from accepting the help of others, or that eventually repulse would-be mentors. Such behaviors, which typically incorporate some form of perceived inadequacy or insecurity, include:

- Appearing weak or intellectually fallible

- Interpreting feedback as disapproval or rejection

- Unwilling to be dependent upon or beholden to another

These barriers to the well-meaning inputs of others not only block learning; they nullify other desirable aspects of mentoring, such as ready access to the mentor's network of associates. The kind leaders we have met through the years avoid such traps that keep them from honing their leadership abilities.

Third, as a part of our interviews, we asked leaders if they ever had a bad boss. "Oh, of course," was the unanimous reply. Most telling, however, was that this confession didn't contain the slightest hint of animosity. Yes, they had endured bad bosses—the arrogant, ill-tempered sort. Yet, remarkably, these leaders learned from them: Thus, whereas it would be a far stretch to describe inadequate managers as exemplary mentors, it would be fair to say that for discriminating people, they served as an occasional model. Our discerning leaders were able to see in these highly compromised people a flicker of respectability. Few individuals are all good or all bad, and while it is easier to notice the goodness in some versus others, those who become great leaders are able to accept a situation as it is and make the best of it, learning what they can, perhaps from a poor leader's analytical genius, penchant for administration, or political wherewithal. If there is anything positive there, a person who is passionate about leading well will find it.

In addition, there always is something to be learned from the dark side. In a *BusinessWeek* article, Keith McFarland referred to negative lessons as "anti-mentoring."[5] In the article, he recalled asking his poor excuse for a boss—the vice president—for a transfer; euphemistically implied in this discussion was that his boss was the reason behind the request. The vice president agreed, on condition that the VP would relay this news to his superior. There was a lot lost in translation. The vice president conveyed that the reason for the unsuspecting employee's request was that the company president was too meddlesome and intrusive in everyday affairs.

From this experience, McFarland learned that people are reliable and consistent. Those who can't be trusted . . . can't be trusted. He mistakenly believed that the vice president would morph from a self-interested, overcontrolling jerk into a congenial and understanding boss. No way. Later he learned another anti-mentoring lesson: you spend too much time at work to spend it with people you don't like or trust. Good leaders are able to learn from both their own and others' mistakes—preferably the latter.

Fourth, as students of history and literature, good leaders adopt both real and fictional heroes and heroines as mentors. Indeed, many of the leaders we spoke to mentioned people like Lord Nelson, Elizabeth I, and Winston Churchill as individuals from whom they derived wisdom and strength and noted memorable books ranging from *Atlas Shrugged* to *Henry IV* as doorways into human nature—and sources of great pleasure. Thus, those who are interested in the craft of leadership cast a wide net throughout history and art, finding role models who inspire. In contrast, those who are only interested in the here and now, who cling only to given ideas and approaches of proven usefulness, will fail to recognize enduring lessons in the historical and literary records.

The remainder of this book focuses on good people who have made business their primary avocation: people who have treated managerial excellence itself as serious business, who have felt the momentousness of leading and worked hard and tirelessly to make organizations successful and work life more satisfying. In subsequent chapters, we describe a category of leader that, in sustaining the aggregate will of groups to continuously move forward, has largely mastered one of the most ancient arts.

One caveat as we begin our exploration: We use the terms *management* and *leadership* interchangeably throughout the text. Our rationale will become clearer as you proceed through the book. But briefly, although these concepts have slightly different connotations, we view the main differences as a matter of degree versus kind: that is, as quantitatively as opposed to qualitatively different.

NOTES

1. Colvin, G. (2007). Power: a cooling trend. *Fortune*, December 10: 13.

2. Drucker, P.F. (1959). *Landmarks of Tomorrow*. London: Heinemann.

3. Wales, J. (2007). How I work: The knowledge maestro. *Fortune*, September 7: 36.

4. Allen, T.D., Eby, L.T., Poteet, M.L., Lentz, E., & Lima, L. (2004). Career benefits associated with mentoring for protégés: A meta-analysis. *Journal of Applied Psychology*, 89: 127–136; Underhill, C.M. (2006). The effectiveness of mentoring programs in corporate settings: A meta-analytical review of the literature. *Journal of Vocational Behavior*, 68: 292–307.

5. McFarland, K.R. (2007). Lessons from the anti-mentor. *BusinessWeek*, June 11: 86.

WHAT KIND LEADERS DO

Enter Lady Macbeth. Reflecting on a witch's prophecy that her husband will become King of Scotland, she wonders if, despite his ambitions, he is too soft, "too full o' th' milk of human kindness," to do what it will take when the current king, Duncan, drops by.

At least since the time of Shakespeare, many have questioned the awkward alliance between kindness and leadership. Although the imperatives of leadership are not as extreme as murder, they may involve decisions that involve doing what is best for the company at the expense of other concerns: decisions, for example, that can cost others their livelihoods or affect the well-being of entire communities. In these situations, kindness is perceived as a self-defeating obstruction.

In this book, we maintain that kindness and leadership are complementary, and that this combination specifically gives a leader a crucial edge. Our conclusions are based on our personal experiences, an understanding of the academic literature, and interviews with many business leaders who have quietly made a difference to their companies, their industries, and, in some cases, their country. We don't pretend that our examination covers all facets of leadership. But we believe our inquiry goes to the heart of what it means to be an effective leader and that our exploration of kindness is a refreshing antidote to the sterility of much leadership theory.

We admittedly had our reservations about using the word *kind* to describe a special sort of leader because it conveys a softness from which many in business recoil, even though it seems odd to distance oneself from such a positive trait. We chose to retain it for three reasons. First, kindness is universally understood as a virtue.[1] It is recognized as an essential ingredient of humaneness regardless of religious or ethnic heritage and has a well-deserved role in human affairs.

Second, it approximates in meaning a set of attributes that we found in successful leaders. No one word can capture everything there is to know about any person, but *kindness* appropriately summarizes a constellation of behaviors we have observed among a group of effective leaders.

Third, the leaders with whom we spoke had no difficulty with the term. Indeed, they rather liked it. As long as we properly explain its meaning, each is very pleased to be called kind.

INDUSTRIAL AGE BOSSES

Kindness is not the first word we associate with business. The image of business still largely includes old scenes from industrial America in the early twentieth century: the age of hard work and tough bosses. As the machines heated, spun, milled, and bore, managerial overlords paced factory floors counting the output and pressing employees to produce more and more. This was not the place for weak-kneed supervisors and executives. Forbearance was not a principle of Taylorism and the new scientific management, which adduced tightly choreographed movements between man and machine.[2] The goal was to keep production lines efficiently moving by any means necessary. The only thing worse than workers who wouldn't work was a soft manager who couldn't make them.

Today, the pressure for unremitting productivity from the forces of fierce competition in the global marketplace continues. New, unforeseen market entrants can suddenly emerge from anywhere in the world with a new technology, better business model, or improved product, to exploit a company's weaknesses and rob it of customers.[3] Meanwhile, traditional competitors are always laying in wait for a missed order, a slip in quality, or a lapse in service. The margin of error is very thin, and befuddled, wishy-washy executives who can't manage to the numbers are expendable. We would agree, but the premises of operational precision, rigorous financial oversight, and market wariness that belie organizational success often lead in an unpromising direction: back to the lords of the shop floor and a falsely constructed ideal of an overly severe leader.

We mistake the need for precision with the need for managerial control, the need for oversight with the need for corporate autocracy, and the need for vigilance with the need for icy objectivity and personal detachment. We conclude that what every business presumably needs is a leader who is calculative, single-minded in the financial purposes of the enterprise, and, perhaps, competitive to a fault: to the point of being overbearingly aggressive and belligerent. In this new age of competitiveness, we assume that managers who are incapable or unwilling to grimly snip away at expenses, to relentlessly push employees, and to be unyieldingly tough are too compromised to succeed in a harsh and unforgiving business world. As our erstwhile leaders did in the industrial age, today's leaders ostensibly, too, must be uncompromisingly and dispassionately focused on the prize of productivity gains and wealth creation for shareholders. Everything else is an investment or expense.

The abiding impression of the modern manager remains haunted by images of past generations of overcontrolling thugs: the new company man or woman who has just the right amount of indifference and interpersonal distance to make the unthinkable possible. He must get people to do their jobs the very best they can—without caring too deeply about their burdens. Whatever semblance of decency that emerges is part of a canned, formulaic concoction designed to get results. Those who are unsuccessful at feigning concern are sent off to communication classes where they are shown how to listen harder and to demonstrate empathic awareness through carefully crafted questions and statements.

Since many employees have had to endure the dismissive and erratic treatment of "shouters" during their tenures, our point is proven by that experience. We have a very long way to go before universal decency prevails within management. Why else would more than twelve states now be contemplating laws that allow workers to sue their bosses for "threatening, intimidating or humiliating" behavior, "repeated infliction of verbal abuse," or "gratuitous sabotage . . . of a person's work performance"? Discriminating against specific groups has been outlawed for some time, but states have now turned their attention to those who have been referred to as "the equal opportunity asshole."[4] These are the managers who indiscriminately abuse everyone. Most disconcerting, however, is that despite living in an era of unprecedented economic progress and scientific enlightenment, management practice remains primitive, with the incidence of bullying in the workplace *increasing*, not decreasing as one might have surmised.[5]

Neither of the authors prefers external regulation and law for influencing behavior. We prefer a positive approach, with voluntary acceptance as a first course of action: that is, a method that convinces managers that there are far more dignified and effective ways to get results than by inculcating scream-and-holler cultures. Winning Super Bowl coach Tony Dungy, for example, doesn't curse, sarcastically chew out players, or rant on the sidelines. He believes he can get his team to compete by calmly providing direction and treating players with respect. Interestingly, this demeanor *prevented* him from getting a head coaching job for many years.[6] We need more Tony Dungys, who, in the process of trying to perfect their own lives, set examples for others.

The real disgrace behind the new state laws under consideration is that too many executives who are in a position to do something about mismanagement within their ranks either don't know what is going on or refuse to do anything about it. Organizational leaders who fail to step in when people need them most are culpable.[7] It may be time, as both the *New York Times* and the *Wall Street Journal* recently announced, for a new type of leader who has cast aside the largesse of ego and exercises power in more humane ways.[8] This is tantamount to removing the crook from the hands of royalty, where it once symbolized authority and dominion, and passing it to the shepherd, where it became a symbol of protection and a humbler, more subtle form of power.[9] The less invasive leadership style symbolized by the shepherd's staff reminds us of a quote attributed to Margaret Thatcher: "Being powerful is like being a lady. If you have to tell people you are, you aren't."

WHAT KINDNESS IS NOT

No, kindness is not a word that spontaneously comes to mind when we think of business, and its acceptance as a workplace virtue is made more quaint by highly salient experiences we have all had with loathsome, capricious bosses who somehow manage to escape detection and, inexplicably, ascend the corporate ladder. The quality we have singled out for study, then, is not an obvious one. Before proceeding further, however, let us briefly say what kindness is *not*, in order to clear up some common misconceptions. As a Latin proverb suggests, giving an account of what something isn't helps to clarify what it is.[10]

There Is More to Personality than Kindness

Leaders exhibit many qualities besides kindness. It is, for example, possible to be hard-nosed and kind, to be cantankerous and kind, to be analytical and kind, or to be gregarious and kind. Kindness comes packaged with many other traits. Thus, leaders' own unique qualities give them a distinctive style. We assert that kindness is part of a good leader's constitution and that others are able to brush aside some of the other qualities that leaders possess in order to see their compassionate centers. Therefore, many different types of people are kind.

We believe that the endless, and tiresome, search for the perfect leadership personality is terribly misguided and ultimately fails to explain what leaders really do and what makes them effective. It is best to think of kindness as a key ingredient in a robust stew. The character of the stew is defined by all of the ingredients in combination, but omit just this one and the fine flavor is lost.

Kind Leaders Aren't Sissies

Part of the problem is that often when we think of people who are kind, they are sometimes overly so—and too much of a good thing is harmful. These individuals are indulgent and naïve; their benevolence is often the target of calculating, homoeconomicus looking for a free ride or easy gain. By kind, we do not mean *sucker* or *pushover*. Nor do we imply a warmly permissive leader whose underlings run wild.

Kindness, like many other traits, has an optimal level that makes it a virtue as opposed to a vice. Too little or too much transforms it into something ugly or suspect. Too much courage can make one fool-hardy, too much pride can make one haughty, too much politeness can make one officious, too much love can make one covetous, and too much kindness can make one a dupe.

Kindness Is Not the Same as Likability

Kindness doesn't preclude a full range of expression, including, at times, displeasure, nor should it be interpreted as excessive amicability. Compare it to the relationship between a parent and child; kindness implies an interpersonal closeness and fondness, but it comes with other baggage. It requires mutual responsibilities that a day at the beach with a buddy does not. This is because parenting goes well beyond common courtesy, the sharing of intimacies, and companionship.

At any given time, a parent can plummet in the likability ratings faster than a discredited televangelist. Parents are supervisors who manage their children with some of the same *modus operandi* as businesses: There are daily responsibilities and performance expectations that are to be executed and met by people with different capabilities, motives, and temperaments. Every day, like it or not, parents are called upon to get the job done. Whereas evaluations of likability may ebb and flow, it is hard to imagine succeeding in this or any interpersonal endeavor without the presumption of kindness to motivate our best intentions and to temper our worst impulses.

As in business, it often is possible for parents to get results without much skill. It is always possible to make people do things through threats of punishment and brute force. But those parents who repeatedly rely upon such measures would hardly be described as "good." Even if such tactics never quite reached the level of abuse, the one-dimensional style is the stuff of satire. Getting results in its various forms is not the sole criterion for parental (or managerial) success. Even so, results fed on a strict diet of fear are fleeting. Children, like employees, are discriminating and know when they are beyond the vigilance and control of others, free to do their own thing (or, in extreme cases, get even)—sometimes in spite of themselves. The goal of leadership is never really to just get results, but to increase the value of the company over time using agreeable means.

The Benefits and Necessity of Kind Leaders

Before we more fully probe what we mean by kindness, let's first consider the effects we want any method of leadership to yield: positive results, to be sure. We would hate for "He's got a great personality" to become a euphemism for poor performance. Additionally, there are four outcomes we think any company would happily endorse.

- Each person works to his maximum capabilities with little slippage in effort over time.

- Each person's capabilities, including moral awareness and aptitude, develop and become more refined over time.

- Each person is willing to exercise her abilities to the fullest in the absence of any immediate contingencies.

- Each person shares a mutual obligation to foster both the personal growth of one another and the collective welfare of the group.

Regardless of whether we are at home or at work, we prize particular qualities in those entrusted with the care of others. These are qualities that can bring out the very best in others by helping them to recognize their unique talents, hone their skills, deliver exceptional—perhaps at times surprising—performance, and remain engaged in the life of the community. Put in this way, leadership, parental, civic, or corporate, doesn't sound so easy and constitutes much more than making decisions on behalf of others and giving orders. Indeed, those leaders who equate leadership with unilateral decision-making and power grossly misunderstand the give-and-take realities of social life and collective action. In order for companies to improve, the people of the organization have to become smarter and more resourceful and work together more effectively over time. For this to occur, people actually have to care about their work, the company, and one another. This requires the expert orchestration of a kind leader.

It has become fashionable lately to envision organizations as amorphous organic entities, along the lines of cells floating in a Petri dish. Each cell—the anthropomorphic person—has its unique code and knows what to do and miraculously combines with other cells to produce higher-order results than one cell could achieve alone. If there is any guidance, it is divine. Self-organization is viewed as a natural process that arises from a few underlying rules and laws, like geese forming a "V" shape to reduce wind resistance and maintain visual contact.

There is no shortage of rhetoric on leaderless groups or, what amounts to the same thing, groups in which everyone is equally conceived as a leader. True, many people are called upon at different times to assume greater authority; we are reminded of Charles Handy's comparison of leadership to the roles and duties found within a rowing crew—who's in charge depends on whether the boat is on or off the river, or whether the crew is racing or training.[11] But the presumption of leaderless or, more accurately, leader-ful groups tends to marginalize the role of one person in charge of it all. It also either fails to recognize or cleverly sidesteps a few simple truths.

- First, most social organizations have some form of hierarchy in which one person has a greater authority than others.[12]

- Second, social organizations contain webs of complex relationships among members who have various talents.

- Third, the people with the authority over the group and with the accountability to achieve specific outcomes must figure out how to best nurture, combine, and use the talents of the group.

- And, fourth, the collective ability of the group must improve with time in order to adapt to new challenges—it has to continuously evolve into a qualitatively better operating unit and effectively react as circumstances change: Put succinctly, the group must learn and develop, *and it is up to the leader to make that happen.*

Even well-meaning, energetic people at times are unable to spontaneously ignite, and a very good reason why a leader is needed in most situations is to light the fuse. Everyone periodically suffers from inertia or self-doubt, is seduced into following an errant course, or becomes distracted. Leaders are needed because we cannot perform optimally without them. It takes a leader with unique abilities to achieve superior results, and we refer to this homogeneous collection of abilities as "kindness."

ACTS OF KINDNESS

Kindness may not have yet caught on within business, but there is plenty of evidence that it is a key component of our evolutionary heritage and instrumental in cooperative, collective behavior. Groups that were able to work effectively together, sometimes requiring sacrifices from individual members, were the ones that outcompeted other groups for resources and thrived.[13] There is even some evidence that a kindness gene has been passed down to us, located on chromosome 7. Missing strands on this chromosome are traceable to Williams syndrome, an affliction that makes those affected indiscriminately and excessively friendly to everyone. Thus, the wisdom of natural selection is that it did not make kindness unconditional.

But it did, in all likelihood, make us especially responsive to the actions of group leaders to whom we look for guidance—those leaders who enhanced the group's welfare by promoting cooperation versus infighting passed along their genetic lineage. Groups that were able to create workable divisions of labor for the benefit of the group *in toto* and unite against warring tribes survived. Thus, the behaviors of successful, prestigious members of groups have a pronounced effect on others, as countless studies on modeling have shown.[14]

The power of modeling is aptly illustrated by a story that is still told about the analytical Robert Rubin, co-CEO at Goldman Sachs, long after his departure. It seems that a senior and a junior member of the firm conceived a novel way to make the company a lot of money and were invited to present their ideas to the management committee. As the senior member of the duo was about to complete the requisite presentation, he was invited by Rubin to step outside the room for a moment. The idea was a good one and there were clear signals it would be adopted, and the senior partner was expecting a special private congratulatory nod from the CEO. Instead, he was told that part of his job was to develop people and that he could have had the more junior person present under his tutelage. So resounding was the message that it remains a part of the lore of Goldman Sachs to this day: help and grow others! This undoubtedly is part of the reason that Goldman Sachs has produced so many fine leaders over the years: Jon Corzine, John Thain, and John White-head, to name just a few.[15]

There also may be a natural foundation for kindness that results from our unusual sensitivity to what is variously known as "reciprocity," "tit-for-tat," and the "Golden Rule." Based on empathy, we treat others in a way we wish to be treated, and others tend to respond in kind. With minor variations, this simple rule goes a long way in facilitating stable cooperation in groups by demonstrating and underscoring the value of mutuality. In his seminal studies using the Prisoner's Dilemma, Axelrod found that in groups where members have mixed motives, it really does pay to be nice.

The Prisoner's Dilemma is an interesting game because it mirrors the quandaries in which many of us find ourselves daily. The game gets its name from the options presented to two crime suspects who have been separated for questioning. Individually, each is motivated to talk in an attempt to receive a lighter sentence; yet, if both talk, then the leverage for a reduced sentence is lost and both are likely to get harsher treatment. If neither talks, both will receive less severe sentences—but not as lenient as the sentence a single confessor would receive. Thus, the dilemma these prisoners face is a familiar one: how to obtain cooperation in groups when there are incentives for individuals to act in self-interest. When the game is played repeatedly over time, those people who settle into a cooperative relationship are those who discover that longer-term gains are best achieved when each player knows the other will act in accordance with their *mutual* interests. In essence, the players realize that doing unto others as they would have others do unto them is not a bad way to do business. Indeed, most of the leaders we spoke with invoked the Golden Rule as their management philosophy, noting that adherence to this principle is the surest way to build close-knit, high-performing communities.

What remains for us in this opening chapter is to briefly describe the specific behaviors that constitute acts of kindness. We propose that kind leaders are *framers, interpreters,* and *enablers* who set clear expectations, provide honest feedback, and promote growth (these behavioral sets are discussed in greater depth in chapters 3 through 5, respectively). The near-term goal is organizational survival by nurturing individuals' development and putting their expanding abilities to good use. The long-term goal is to produce individuals with the requisite capacities to lead by instilling those qualities that permit chronic expressions of kindness (the main subject of chapter 6).

Leaders as Framers

For a moment, let's return to parenting and the good parent. Neither author is by any means an authority on the subject of raising children, having ourselves learned by our own trial and error experiences. But we can say with some confidence that the starting point for kindness is a passionate concern for our children's success. Success is never guaranteed, but there are things parents can do to improve the odds. One thing we can do is define the contours of acceptable and unacceptable behaviors. In order to reduce the confusing array of possible actions, it is helpful to delineate a more manageable space of "shoulds" that enable those around us to thrive. These behaviors are specific to the environment and are designed to improve the chances for success in that place. This framework specifies what you can and cannot do; what is expected and what is not. Similarly, good leaders establish clear boundaries, standards of conduct, and challenging goals that everyone must strive to meet.

Michael Cherkasky, the unpretentious former CEO of Marsh & McLennan, maintains that the distinguishing characteristic of an excellent leader is an ability to identify what is most important from the range of issues that are vying for attention. There isn't much latitude in today's competitive marketplace to squander energy and resources on nonessential or less important directives. His admonition: Focus on the real problems and pursue them with stubborn zeal. Unstated is the critical self-examination required to jettison ideas that aren't worth saving.

The idea behind orienting frameworks is that they provide employees with interpretative guidelines and structures that are automatically initiated as events unfold. They offer a means to understand what is transpiring, the relative importance of information (both present and missing), cues to the most appropriate action to take, and the likely consequences should some things happen or not happen as expected. An organizing schema of "We are a community" elicits certain expectations and reactions to events that a schema of "It's everybody for herself" would not.

EXPECTATIONS MATTER
Kindness does not allow us to founder on indefiniteness, to encounter life without expectations, or to act without purpose or direction. Kindness gives us focus.

Leaders as Interpreters

When people—children or adults—engage in any meaningful activity, sometimes things turn out well and sometimes they don't. Performances can be exemplary or subpar, and for those who want to improve, there are inevitable experiences with both positive and negative outcomes. Usually some form of self-appraisal follows these perfor-mances, based on past experiences, social comparisons, outside inputs, and such. Success depends on developing accurate interpretations of per-formance and the reasons or causes for it. It is simply impossible to excel if an individual repeatedly miscalculates how well or poorly he is doing and is unable to attribute results to the appropriate influences. You don't improve if you falsely believe that you are performing at peak, or that cir-cumstances are conspiring against you and there is nothing you can do other than appeal to fate. A leader's job is to "keep it real": to help oth-ers make sense of their efforts and results and to understand how and why things have gone right or wrong.

We have found that one of the unkindest things a leader can do is cover for poor performance either with faint praise or by avoiding the issue altogether. Absolutely no good comes from acquiescing to performances that fall below expectations. High performers are frus-trated and angered by incompetence in their midst, low performers repeatedly suffer failure, and the leader's judgment is questioned and credibility threatened throughout the organization. Once it is under-stood that poor performers suck the life out of companies, truthful-ness becomes a much easier and salient option.

Poor leaders not only can pad the truth when interpreting indi-viduals' performances, but also can turn a blind eye to the organiza-tion as a whole—frequently with more dire consequences. There are many ways of obfuscating the truth in organizations, but authors Ol-son and van Bever capture the most virulent form, which they call the three-part psychology of paralysis.[17]

As applied to companies such as Kodak, Caterpillar, and Sears, Ol-son and van Bever propose that the psychology of self-deception con-sists of equal parts of disdain for the competition, denial of threat, and rationalization of the current course of action by invoking false assump-tions about customers, competitors, and markets. As a consequence, all these companies witnessed the gradual, ultimately dramatic erosion of their revenues and privileged industry positions.

Jay Ireland, the charming and self-effacing president and CEO of GE Asset Management, makes much the same point when reflecting on group and individual performance metrics. Using the apt metaphor of boiling a frog to death by gradually turning up the heat in increments not sensed by the frog, Ireland periodically takes the pot off the stove to test the water temperature, making certain it hasn't gotten too hot. He realizes that people easily can be seduced into thinking everything is all right when it truly isn't. Periodic assessments that ensure that the company is evaluating the situation correctly and making the right measurements help to guard against performance-related falsehoods and future surprises.

> **THE TRUTH MATTERS**
> It would not be kind for leaders to allow others to persist in a world of untruths by misrepresenting how they, others, or the company are actually doing—good or bad. Kind leaders endorse reality.

Leaders as Enablers

It is personally gratifying to be an expert and tempting to showcase that status by repeatedly showing others how to perform their jobs, sometimes redoing the work of others in one's own style. Of course, any new complex activity requires some show-and-tell and closely observed practice. Yet, as agonizing as it is to watch those we care about risk failure, there is no way to encourage growth and personal fulfill-

ment other than to allow them to make decisions and try out new behavioral repertoires without second-guessing them along the way.
The path to independence is engineered by leaders who carefully prepare the ground ahead until followers are ready to choose a direction
on their own. The only way to expand and refine employees' capabilities is to periodically test their skills.

There is much uncertainty in business, and it would be foolish to
believe otherwise. No worthy leader moves forward with absolute
surety that he will succeed. If he does, sooner or later he is guaranteed
to be disappointed. Instead, he moves ahead with conviction, preparedness, and confidence, knowing that his attempts—even errant
ones—will make him better. That is, the process of ongoing improvement matters more than reaching a destination.

John Pepper, the former CEO of Procter & Gamble, now chairman
of the board at Disney, suggests just that in pointing to the slogan
Procter & Gamble (P&G) lives by: "Find a better way." Clothing designer Eileen Fisher communicates much the same through the motif
of a flowing river. To Eileen Fisher, "We are in the river" means continuous learning, continuous change, continuous advancement. The
cultural norm is to be restlessly inquisitive and to promote the commitment to action, supported by the conviction that smart people will
find their way and help to direct the company into the future. This is
essentially the philosophy of the supercharged CEO of Tupperware,
Rick Goings: Hire well, give the talent some elbow room, and create
conditions in which they can productively feed off one another.

Successful companies often operate a little like the lost wartime
Hungarian patrol.[18] Lost in the Alps, a member of the team miraculously discovered a map in his pocket, and the group managed to hike
to safety. The group subsequently discovered that the map was of the
Pyrenees, not the Alps. Nonetheless, confident in their abilities to
find an escape route, competent climbers and orienters notice clues,

make objective determinations of fact, jointly learn as they progress, and make ongoing plans accordingly.

There is a fine line that the best leaders are able to draw. On the one hand, they are terribly unsettled and dissatisfied with the status quo. This comes through loud and clear from leaders such as Vanguard founder Jack Bogle, who has made a career of rabble-rousing and challenging investment companies to modify managerial and financial practices that rob investors of their due returns. On the other hand, such leaders remain remarkably upbeat about the future. They do not allow themselves to be encumbered by imperfections and incapacitated by despair, but plow ahead despite the obstacles. This requires a great deal of courage, energy, and endurance in order to cope with the inevitable setbacks.

GROWTH MATTERS
It would not be kind for leaders to shelter others from errors and mistakes simply because they cannot tolerate the discomfort associated with setbacks or temporary imprecision—the ultimate goal is to develop the potential in others and inspire action. Kind leaders facilitate growth.

Thus, kind leaders have special advantages because their outlook allows them to establish acceptable standards of conduct, foster abilities in a conducive setting, promote the spontaneous exercise of employees' faculties, and stimulate risk-taking and stretch performances, often in the service of organizational change.

At this point, we should temper the analogy of parenting to leadership, since there are many aspects of familial relationships that set them apart from those found in business. For example, even kids with severe behavior problems aren't fired from the family, nor do we advocate the same degree of paternalism found in close family relationships for organizations—those types of protection are long gone from the corporate scene. Instead, we suggest that managing performance has parallels with family management and that organizational results can be achieved within a climate of tolerance, patience, empathy, and kindness. Indeed, we submit that these results are of higher quality and are more stable and enduring over the long term than those attained through other means.

There are good reasons for these superior results, built upon the simple premise that most people are competent and would prefer to do better than worse. A foundational belief of the kind leaders with whom we visited is that everyone wants to excel and grow, and that there is a force of human nature that propels individuals to do their best. That force can be sidetracked only by circumstance, including the disruptive influences of lousy leaders. If you do not believe that—if you think that people are inherently lazy, incapable dullards who dislike challenge and responsibility—this book will be of no help to you.

What recourse is available to help the unwilling and unable? The unable have to be closely monitored at all times, and their jobs have to be narrowly defined in order to be easy to learn and to minimize decision-making and error. This is in contrast to the entrepreneurial spirit of Home Depot founders Bernie Marcus and Arthur Blank and their idea of a job being enclosed by an invisible fence: Feel free to roam around some; when you wander too far afield from your job responsibilities, you'll get a warning that you are about to be zapped. As people successfully push toward the outermost boundaries, the fence is moved farther away and job duties are expanded.[19]

The unwilling have to be goaded to work through a mixture of incentives, tied to units of outputs and quotas, and penalties, tied to nonperformance in its many guises, e.g., absenteeism. The only learning that goes on in these environments involves employees scheming how to get the most for the least—thereby confirming the very human nature that the organizational society rests upon. This is a vicious cycle that goes nowhere, circling round and round in an endless, exhausting succession of moves and countermoves. Those who have been trapped within such a closed system know all too well that once the cycle is established, it is extremely hard to break free. As a result, key competencies are never passed on to subsequent generations of leaders, cementing managerial ineptitude and dysfunctional relationships for many years to come.

SAFE LEADERS, TOUGH LOVE

Leaders, we should add, do not build character by being unconditionally nice. Positive regard is wonderful, but we have been in organizations that are exceptionally chummy and suffer from what we refer to as the "delusion of niceness." These are places where it is impolite to offend, impolitic to disagree, and impertinent to ask others to go out of their way: exceedingly sweet places, but extremely stale. Lucy Kellaway, in her weekly *Financial Times* column, has referred to the excessive, incessant positivity in corporations as "spiritual spam" and the resulting cultures as "cults of yes."[20] The most obvious drawback to such environments is that nothing substantive ever seems to get accomplished, save for readily solvable problems such as simple cost-cutting measures or rote manipulations of prices. The deeper underlying issue, however, is that the people within these environments are unable to learn because the cheery, upbeat outlook promoted as a way to sustain morale and productivity makes people hopelessly unreflective. The steep price for contentment is to shrink from the glaring imperfections of the company. Those "negative" people who point out the flaws just aren't with the program.[21]

The fact is, kindness isn't always nice. It pushes others to do better; it asks them to try out things that they are uncertain they can accomplish; it requires them to engage in activities that they are not sure they will like. Another fact is this: Folks don't always take kindly to kindness. Leaders, even great ones, cannot save everybody. People do not enter the workplace as identical employees. As such, employees—people—are more or less open to what leaders have to offer. Of course, people can be led without any pretense of a relationship, but not in the way we have in mind, and not in the way that is most valuable to organizations. For that, a certain degree of receptivity is required.

No leader worth his or her salt will immediately assume that employees will uniformly respond to the same motivational techniques or give themselves over to the leader's commands to the same degree. People differ in how cautiously they approach and enter new relationships. Some plunge in head first; some dip their toes. But leaders understand that everyone—no matter how tentative—must eventually be assured that the waters are safe.

When coaching executives, Timothy Habbershon, at the Arthur M. Blank Center for Entrepreneurship at Babson College, asks a simple question: "Are you a safe person?"[22] The answer amplifies a great deal about the health of an organization, since safe people are approachable. Employees will alert such company leaders to problems, offer constructive suggestions and advice, and make decisions unafraid of what might befall them as a consequence. Unsafe leaders instill fear, use the power of their positions to influence, never solicit advice from others, and when suggestions are offered, promptly dismiss them—politely or impolitely—as immaterial. Kindness makes leaders safe.

Kindness can be perceived as genuine only in environments that are temporally durable and interpersonally reliable. The presumption is that the relationship will last, and that its rules of engagement are trust and respect. The intangibles that hold the leader-follower relationship together mean that each has the long-term welfare of the other at heart and neither wishes to disappoint. No ostensible act of kindness will measure up if there is widespread disbelief that a person's interests really matter. Thus, and as we indicate throughout the book, our kind leaders work hard to establish cultures that allow others to accept unfamiliar assignments, corrective feedback, and rigorous goals with open minds, assuring that these actions are taken with clear purposes—invariably to make the individual and the organization better.

NOTES

1. Seligman, M.E.P., Steen, T.A., Park, N., & Peterson, C. (2005). Positive psychology progress. *American Psychologist*, 60: 410–421.

2. Taylor, F.W. (2006). *The Principles of Scientific Management*. Fairfield, IA: 1st World Library Literary Society.

3. These are the types of conditions that Christensen has addressed: Christensen, C.M. (1997). *The Innovator's Dilemma: When New Technologies Cause Great Firms to Fail*. Cambridge, MA: Harvard Business School Press; Christensen, C.M., & Raynor, M.E. (2003). *The Innovator's Solution: Creating and Sustaining Successful Growth*. Cambridge, MA: Harvard Business School Press.

4. Fisher, D. (2007). Bully police. *Forbes*, September 3, p. 50; Legal notes (2004). *BusinessWeek*, May 14: 14.

5. Hodson, R., Roscigno, V.J., & Lopez, S.H. (2006). Chaos and the abuse of power: Workplace bullying in organizational and interactional context. *Work and Occupations*, 33: 382–416.

6. Hymowitz, C. (2007). Two football coaches have a lot to teach screaming managers. *Wall Street Journal*, January 29: B1.

7. Poorly organized work conditions and laissez-faire leadership have been implicated in hundreds of cases of bullying; see Leymann, H. (1996). "The content and development of mobbing at work," *European Journal of Work and Organizational Psychology*, 5: 165–184.

8. Schwartz, N.D. (2007). C.E.O. evolution phase 3. *New York Times*, November 10: B1; Murray, A. (2007). After the revolt: Creating a new CEO. *Wall Street Journal*, May 5: A1.

9. Diamond, J.A. (2006). Maimonides on kingship: The ethics of imperial humility. *Journal of Religious Ethics*, 34: 89–114.

10. As cited in Lorand, R. (1994). Beauty and its opposites. *Journal of Aesthetics and Art Criticism*, 52: 399–406.

11. Handy, C. (1996). The new language of organizing and its implications for leaders. In F. Hesselbein, M. Goldsmith, & R. Beckhard (eds.): *Leader of the Future*. San Francisco: Jossey-Bass.

12. Jaques, E. (1990). In praise of hierarchy. *Harvard Business Review*, January-February: 127–133.

13. This conjecture and the discussion that immediately follows can be found in Judson, O. (2007). The selfless gene. *Atlantic*, October: 90.

14. There are countless studies that document the power of observational learning, but the famous Bobo doll experiments by Bandura and colleagues documented that power on film and raised new questions and areas of research; see Bandura, A., Ross, D., & Ross, S.A. (1961). Transmission of aggression through imitation of aggressive models. *Journal of Abnormal and Social Psychology*, 63: 575–582.

15. Weber, J. (2006). The leadership factory. *BusinessWeek*, June 12: 60.

16. In addition to the original studies by Axelrod (see Axelrod, R., & Dion, D. (1988). The further evolution of cooperation. *Science*, 242: 1385–1390; Axelrod, R., & Hamilton, W.D. (1981). The evolution of cooperation. *Science*, 211: 1390–1396), several more recent papers in *Sci-*

ence have similarly examined the evolution of cooperation: Boyd, R., & Matthew, S. (2007). Behavior: A narrow road to cooperation. *Science*, 1858–1859; Gürerk, O., Irlenbusch, B., & Rockenbach, B. (2006). The competitive advantage of sanctioning institutions. *Science*, 312: 108–111; Henrich, J. (2006). Cooperation, punishment, and the evolution of human institutions. *Science*, 312: 60–61; Nowak, M.A. (2006). Five rules for the evolution of cooperation. *Science*, 314: 1560–1563.

17. Olson, M.S., & Van Bever, D. (2008). *Stall Points: Most Companies Stop Growing—Yours Doesn't Have To.* New Haven, CT: Yale University Press.

18. Weick, K.E. (1987). Substitutes for strategy. In D.J. Teece (ed.): *The Competitiveness Challenge: Strategies for Industrial Innovation and Renewal.* Cambridge, MA: Ballinger.

19. Marcus, B., & Blank, H. (2000). The invisible fence. In P. Krass (ed.) *The Book of Management Wisdom,* New York: John Wiley & Sons.

20. Kellaway, L. (2007). Just say "no" to the new managerial cult of yes. *Financial Times*, July 23: 10.

21. Argyris nicely describes this dynamic in Argyris, C. (1994). Good communication that blocks learning. *Harvard Business Review*, July-August: 77–85.

22. Habbershon, T.G. (2006). Are you safe? *BusinessWeek (SmallBiz)*, Fall: 18.

WHO KIND LEADERS ARE

In a recent commencement address, the chief executive officer of McCoy Corporation (a building and supply company headquartered in Texas), Brian McCoy, talked about success and recounted the following story.[1] A young store manager had approached him several years earlier seeking advice on what he should do to be successful. McCoy offered what he now describes as a woefully inadequate suggestion: "Well, you've got to work really hard." The necessity of hard work is hardly in dispute as a prerequisite, but with the benefit of time and wisdom, he now believes that the wrong question was asked and answered. The question is not what you should *do* to be successful, but *who you need to become.*

This recast question underscores the importance of character to success and broadens what it means to be successful by incorporating character into its definition. Warren Buffett summed it up best in mentioning three things required for success: integrity, intelligence, and energy. He adds that if you are missing the first, the other two will kill you.[2] That is, success can't be unqualified; it must be guided by conscience so that both the end results and the person achieving them are worthy of respect.

PERSONAL CONNECTION, NOT CHARISMA

The modern idea of charisma comes from the political economist and sociologist Max Weber, who viewed it as a divine gift—consistent with the original Greek meaning—that imbued those who had it with great influence through the power of their personalities.[3] Charisma, indeed, has biblical allusions traceable to the Apostle Paul's list of "charisms," such as the power to speak in tongues and work miracles. Today's more secular version, following Weber, emphasizes a host of traits that enables leaders to vividly, passionately, and authoritatively communicate a vision of the future that captures both the attention and the allegiance of others. More plainly, we'd say that these people are "dynamic."[4]

Our society places great value on charisma; we routinely tune in to the myriad television shows and news reports that spotlight actors and politicians who emit an alluring glow. Often, we want to be just like them. If you happen to be charismatic, great, but that isn't the signature characteristic of a great leader. We think kindness is.

Yes, a great leader has to be able to organize his thoughts, communicate exceptionally well, and have some sense of drama to be effective, but he needs something more to get the words to resonate with others. The words have to be spoken by someone who is concerned about you, who understands what you need and want for yourself, and who is unafraid to reveal that he or she—like you—is a member of the human race. There is a perverted assumption that circulates among the managerial ranks that one must maintain psychological distance from others to be an effective leader. In fact, the opposite is true. The effectiveness of leaders emanates from a common worldview and bond. There is a basic connection among people, who all fundamentally want the same things: to be appreciated, to belong, to feel good about themselves, to make a difference.

Kindness is an apropos term to apply to leadership because it implies precisely such root connections among people engaged in mean-

ingful, reciprocal relationships. Those relations are cultivated and reinforced by six virtues, which we view as the ingredients of kindness,
that place encounters within the workplace in context:

- Compassion

- Integrity

- Gratitude

- Authenticity

- Humility

- Humor

As we begin our discussion of the various elements of kindness,
bear in mind that these are not optional character traits that are simply nice to have, but are required if you want to be an effective leader.

COMPASSION

Though compassion has been called *the* most basic social emotion, it
isn't readily associated with the workplace.[5] Yet to purposely bar compassion from leadership's repository, one would have to believe that the
personal concern implied by compassion has no curative or restorative
powers: that people will not perform any better or worse in its absence.
Since just about every leader we spoke with mentioned compassion as
necessary for organizational effectiveness, it is worth exploring their
rationales. But first a story.[6]

A heart surgeon, attended by an entourage of residents and medical
students, visited a seriously injured patient he had recently operated

upon. The patient had attempted suicide by jumping from a window high enough from the ground to do major damage, but not high enough to kill. The surgeon admired his handiwork, nodded approvingly, and remarked that there were better ways to punish oneself than jumping off buildings—like taking up golf. The entourage laughed. The patient lay still in anguish. Later, the surgeon espoused his philosophy to his trainees: Given the choice between a straight cut and taking the time to show care, he would choose the straight cut any day.

This story nicely illustrates the following (false) assumption: Technique trumps relationships. We often buy into this sort of argument— we know that compassion won't restore blood flow through the heart or close up wounds. This assumption requires a scenario in which everyone is expected to just do their jobs. If they do them efficiently and effectively, all will be fine. The doctor is expected to perform the surgery, the students are expected to learn, and the patient is expected to heal. The results achieved will be based on physiological fact, and the connections among the parties and the emotional state of the patient will have no bearing on outcomes. Impugn the dignity of the patient with a callous joke—no problem. Clearly, this is all wrong. The entire rehabilitative process will depend on the will of the patient, and that, in turn, will depend a great deal on what caregivers, including the surgeon, say and do.

Compassion in the workplace matters because it provides employees with that extra amount of strength they need to perform, whether it's overcoming personal problems, trouble at home, or job-specific challenges. But in order to provide the type of support that may be needed, the would-be leader first needs to imagine what someone who is in pain is going through. That is, the leader needs to have empathy: to understand what another is feeling and care enough to do something about it. There have been many definitions of emotional intelligence, but they all generally converge on empathic awareness of others' affective states, as well as one's own, and leadership excellence partially depends on an ability to use those cues to stimulate appropriate action.[7]

Fortunately, most of us have been raised with an ability to place ourselves in another's position and to view the world through her eyes. But sometimes we get disconnected from the plights of others and become unduly insular in our outlook. Success and hubris can get in the way. Most of the time, though, the reason is much simpler and more innocent. Leaders become increasingly isolated from the employees in the trenches and, come to think of it, their customers. As in Plato's cave, in which people are only able to see shadows of passersby on walls, the higher in the organization executives move, the less they see of real people. Their reality becomes second-order representations, financial reports, and the words of others, who very well may be obsequious, self-serving sycophants (abundantly reviled by the leaders in our study and to be shunned at all costs).

The leadership remedy is to stay in touch with those who work for you so that you get to know the people and what they are up against. One simple solution is to leave the executive suite and venture into the field, remaining accessible to the rank and file. Whatever happened to managing by walking around?

A second solution is to ask executives to work at an operational job under the tutelage of the employee in that position, as, for example, Smucker's does as part of its new employee orientation program. There is no finer way to understand the guts of the operations, the nature of the work, and employees' perspectives than standing in their shoes.

Finally, there is leadership training. Not the kind that instructs on how to empathize—good luck with that—but the kind that incorporates the need for empathy within the natural borders of leadership. We are thinking of what the former chief operating officer of the U.S. Marine Corps, General Martin Steele, told us about the training of Marines. The modern Marine needs three hearts to be effective in urban combat: (1) a warm heart to interact compassionately with the populace; (2) a diplomatic heart to help ease tensions on the street; and (3) the warring heart that is prepared to fight when there is no other recourse.

Compassion provides the motivation to help, presenting the leader with an array of options to pursue, from doing nothing to employing various mentoring tactics, such as soothing and encouraging, guiding and coaching, and teaching and demonstrating—all legitimate support mechanisms in one circumstance or another. There is no textbook solution other than to follow one's instincts regarding what the situation calls for. However, you will be more likely to choose wisely if you keep the ultimate goal of any compassionate response in mind: to promote improvement while preserving personal dignity. Sometimes "I'm sure you can figure it out," sometimes "Here, let me show you," and sometimes "You have to lean in more toward the plate and use your wrists when you swing" will be the appropriate course. Compassion is an instructive guide.

INTEGRITY

All of the leaders to whom we spoke stated that character counts in leadership and that integrity is one of its central ingredients, as you might imagine. Most said it was *the* chief ingredient, which conforms to research results in which integrity is cited most frequently by executives as the cornerstone of ethical leadership.[8] *Integrity* frequently appears in corporate mission and value statements, even within ugly, ethically suspect companies. As Jack Bogle says, "One hundred percent of CEOs will tell you that integrity matters, but a

much smaller percent mean it." The poster child for moral hypocrisy—
as it is for so many other wrongs—is none other than Enron. It boasted
of rectitude while ripping off shareholders. But it has plenty
of disreputable company, and while most CEOs say they value
integrity, surveys show that less than 50 percent of employees believe it.[9]

The distinguishing feature of companies that espouse integrity is
that they make it clear that it really matters, and they are prepared to
act on their principles. Chief executives typically think about integrity in slightly different ways, but we can sum up their common
understandings by way of analogy. Not too long ago, a heavily used
bridge in Minneapolis spanning the Mississippi River collapsed, with
tragic results. Engineers would say that the bridge lacked integrity.[10]
If it had integrity, its design and construction would meet the needs
it was intended to fulfill, reliably, consistently, and predictably. A
bridge has integrity, then, when its parts have been assembled in a
fashion that ensures the utmost in stability and quality, and it meets
our expectations of what bridges are supposed to do: safely convey a
load from one side to the other.

People with integrity are similarly solid, doing what people are
supposed to do: They reliably, consistently, and predictably act on
a set of values that ensures safety in interpersonal encounters. They
keep promises and confidences, remain forthright and nonevasive, and
are unbiased and even-handed.

The leaders of high-integrity cultures are aware that people, even
those with scruples, sometimes succumb to temptation and that one
major ethical slip from an employee in a responsible position can cost
a company millions of dollars, its independence, or its life. They also
know that most of what people do in organizations is done outside of
the vigilance of others—a good number of companies these days have
over 100,000 employees. Most decisions are made when no one is

watching. So they understand that they have to take precautions so that the companies they build remain ones of great integrity.

By synthesizing research results and our interviewees' methods, we are able to offer a three-point prescription for the sound construction of integrity in organizations.

Hire for Character, Never for Convenience

It is far easier to bring in people who subscribe to your belief system than to try to influence behavior after the fact. Thus, companies that truly understand the character of their employees to be a competitive advantage spend a lot of time getting to know candidates before they let them in. The recruitment and hiring processes are seen as being as fundamental as any other operating procedures, and they are well planned, thorough, and to be taken seriously by everyone involved.

The need for a careful selection process applies to any population where cohesiveness and the interpersonal experiences of group members are crucial for superior performance. For example, when the perceptive, farsighted Dan Ritchie became chancellor at the University of Denver, he instituted admissions procedures that required interviews. Today, 6,000 three-on-one interviews are conducted in thirty-three cities in order to fill 1,100 spots. The university quite reasonably wants to recruit students not only on the basis of their academic achievements but on the basis of their character, because it wants to create an engaging, enjoyable, and memorable learning environment where the students can perform at their best and grow. Applications at the university are up by 48 percent.

To us, the many virtues of diligent selection seem self-evident, but then again, the majority of companies we have observed over the years are very desperate to fill vacancies with bodies in order to get the work done. These companies don't see the forest for the trees and believe that just any tree will thrive in the local habitat.

As an important aside, hiring for values does not undermine a company's desire for diversity, regarding either demographic profiles or ideas. There is an important balancing act that good companies perform with regard to hiring, development, and diversity. The broader goal is to infuse new ideas and multiple perspectives into the company while maintaining the core value system and sense of organizational continuity. That is, the goal is to keep the company fresh without destroying its historical grounding and basic belief system. In general, companies achieve this balance by having a "promote-from-within" policy. Such a policy develops and replenishes the ranks through a carefully managed career progression, but selectivity fills key spots when there are no suitable internal candidates (as ascertained by the performances of candidates, not job tenure), or when it is recognized that new skills and outlook would add value. Microsoft is currently struggling with this very issue. Historically a great developer of in-house management talent, it has recently elected to go outside to fill key positions, hiring new leaders for its online advertising and videogame groups.[11] A similar logic holds for boards of directors: It is important to seed the board with qualified people who have diverse points of view and unique insights into the future directions of the company.

Correct Mistakes Quickly

Whereas there is some tolerance for temporary performance-related failings, hiring errors associated with chronic underperformance, poor cultural fit, or severe violations of the corporate code of ethics are unfailingly remedied swiftly—a couple of our leaders bemoaned "not quickly enough." The former CFO of GE recently described just how far GE would go to preserve the integrity and reputation of the company.[12] Certainly, those who knowingly and recklessly violated company rules were terminated. But the cultural failures of leadership were also punished. For example, there were instances of fraud and graft when dealing with foreign governments within one of the divisions that were known to many and persisted for a prolonged period of time: shady behaviors that were overlooked. When these practices came to light, an internal investigation found that the leaders of the respective areas were unaware of what was happening. Yet they still were found culpable—with others—for permitting a badly broken culture to survive and thrive in the corporate netherworld, and they were fired. Such broad-based wrongdoing that persisted over time could not be excused.

Michael Cherkasky faced a similar dilemma when he took over at Marsh & McLennan. All parts of the company reeled from government investigation into the company, which spotlighted untoward practices, including frequent contingency fees (i.e., bribes to secure business). Cherkasky rapidly moved to wipe out any unseemly practices and to transform a culture that formerly tolerated them. One routine he instituted involved commonsense *gut checks* throughout the organization: Upon review, if a practice isn't consistent with the organization's values, don't do it, or fix it immediately, letting all parties know what has occurred and what will be done.

Live the Values

All of us receive cues from our environment about what is advisable or inadvisable, appropriate or inappropriate, good or bad, right or wrong. We are programmed to be quick learners and keen observers of others. The words of leaders resound, and their actions have tremendous influence on what employees regard as acceptable. This all makes perfect sense: Actions really do "speak" more loudly than words. A leader who obviously acts in ways inconsistent with the norms and values of the organization will be scorned by employees as a corporate hypocrite, while subtly inviting those with a passion for self-interest to join him in similar violations.

For our leaders, however, living a values-based life isn't confined to the corporate setting. Watchful eyes are always on the leader, and good companies realize that. In addition, behaving ethically is habit-forming: Repetition solidifies one's ethical armor, making the temptations we all are presented with less enticing. Leaders, then, are expected to show the same equanimity, honor, and grace in all facets of life. As Michael Critelli, the scholarly chairman of Pitney Bowes, put it, that includes demonstrating integrity in all of the little things, from making accurate declarations of goods when traveling internationally to paying one's taxes and accurately completing expense reports. The exhortation is to practice integrity everywhere and always, in order to make it a habit.

True leaders would be the first to acknowledge that they have flaws like everyone else, but nevertheless understand that the character of a leader and what he or she expresses are intimately connected. It is possible for a person's character to get in the way of the message. How well would you be able to hear what a leader has to say if you discovered that he spends his spare time viewing pornographic materials of children in his office? There are scenes in *Downfall* (Sony Pictures, 2005) in which Hitler, his henchmen, and their spouses—who have retreated to their bunker under the German Chancellery in Berlin as the war closes in around them—are served a very nice dinner. It is hard to view these scenes without feeling utter disgust and vicariously choking on the food. The same meal prepared elsewhere and served in more congenial company would taste pretty good. The point is this: If leaders lose credibility because of suspect morals, it doesn't matter what they serve, since they will have a hard time finding people who will voluntarily consume it.

Ultimately, a message is only as reliable as the source, and that makes credibility a central component of leadership integrity. You won't follow a message if you don't believe, or believe in, the speaker. Credible leaders are those with great moral conviction and high ethical standards who, in the shorthand of leadership theorists Kouzes and Posner, follow the credo, DWYSYWD: Do What You Say You Will Do.[13] The importance of credibility was confirmed by every leader with whom we spoke: Without credibility, forget about leading.

There are three requirements for credibility.[14] First, have a history of follow-through. That works in two ways: doing what you say you will do, and making sure that what you said was important actually gets done. Too many leaders have a tendency to "forget," and then employees no longer take them seriously.

The second requirement is expertise. If others think you are managerially or technically inept, then they won't believe that you will do what you say because they won't think you can. This simple prescription sometimes gets lost in the theoretical thicket, but demonstrating competence is a must.

The third requirement concerns trust, and we would like to linger on this topic for a moment. Every reader of this book realizes that companies that are able to build trust have certain advantages. In particular, interpersonal trust greatly reduces transaction costs in social relations. If you trust people, you are confident that they will competently meet expectations inherent to the relationship and fulfill commitments made, and you need nothing more than their assurance that what needs to get done, will. No need for inordinate amounts of oversight, ad nauseam progress reports, or initiation of parallel projects, just in case. Everything works more efficiently when there is trust, and trust is predicated on the good character of the people at the top of the organizational chart.

If you imagine what life would be like without trust, then you have a clue to a second advantage of organization-wide trust. It fosters cooperation, and since organizations are cooperative enterprises, that makes it essential. Distrust, on the other hand, is fuel for unhealthy conflict and infighting. Without trust, there are rampant suspicions pertaining to one another's motives and an uneasy sense that one is always being victimized. And, of course, if you are vigilant for slights and injustices, you will be sure to find them. There isn't much good-natured helping or citizenship in such corrosive environments.

If you are a leader and want to build a culture of trust and remain credible, then you can't hedge on what you say or parse words—that's the advice from our leaders, and it makes sense. Developing trust among employees, suppliers, and customers entails adhering to commitments, even though conditions may have changed and your obligations will cost you money. If a company means that trust is conditional on the company's always coming out ahead, then don't expect much reciprocity from the workforce or others. Eileen Fisher recently held back a new clothing design for several months even though it had reached the production stage because "it wasn't quite right yet." It is tempting to renege on expensive commitments and to rationalize the decision, e.g., the customer won't know the difference, but regardless, Eileen Fisher would rather bear the cost of a product she was dissatisfied with than go to market and possibly sever trust with the company's customers.

Similarly, in a revealing story of customer-centric Amazon, *New York Times* writer Joe Nocero explains how Amazon replaced a Playstation 3 he had ordered for his son free of charge, and without the rigmarole of fighting through several organizational layers for approval. It's a long story, but it's one in which Amazon is blameless regarding why the customer never received his initial order, but made him whole nonetheless.[15]

Companies leave evidence all the time indicating what kind of company they are and how much trust others should place in them. For example, we recall the time a newly hired employee notified the company that he would be unable to start work on the appointed date because his mother had died. The company could easily have accepted a delayed starting day. But that's not what the company did. It advised the employee of its grieving policy and said that it would be possible for him to begin as planned *and* attend to his personal matters—with pay. Companies that do the honorable thing are repaid a hundredfold by employees who understand that their interests are a part of the business equation.

The depth of thoughtfulness, caring, and sacrifice required to build trust is vividly illustrated by the actions of Lieutenant Colonel Hal Moore during a ferocious three-day siege in the Ia Drang Valley in Vietnam. Although his battalion was significantly outnumbered, he was the first off the helicopter and into the battle and the last back on after all of his men had been accounted for. During the battle, he refused an order to return to high command for a briefing, in order to stay with his men. We think it is easy to trust someone who clearly shows that there isn't anything more important than the welfare of the people under his command and is personally invested in ensuring it.[16]

GRATITUDE

Many of the leaders we spoke with live what most of us would regard as average lives. It is true that "rich or poor, it's nice to have money,"[17] but based on our casual observations, you won't find the conspicuous trappings of privilege in this group. By and large, they live in the homes they have always lived in, have the spouses they have always had, vacation in the places to which they always have gone, and value the long-standing friendships they have made. In other words, they are content with what they have—and very thankful for it. They periodically stop to savor all that life has to offer and to find meaning and possibility in their daily regimen, when less noble souls may sense only futility and boredom.

We have observed that kind leaders have *gratitude*.[18] We describe its specific role in quality leadership below, but first a few words on gratitude itself. To be grateful is to realize that one's life story includes many important characters, good *and* bad, and that one has benefited from the goodwill and sacrifices of others. We never probed religious beliefs, but we suspect that, in some cases at least, this thankfulness to others extends to God or other nonhuman agents such as fate. Indeed, good leaders see themselves as very fortunate people.

In addition to having a sense of abundance and an aptitude to derive pleasure from the little things in life, gratitude is also revealing of an attitude. There are many benevolent people out there, and what has always struck us is how some people are more receptive to generosity than others. Fundamentally, in order to receive the gift of kindness, you have to accept that you cannot succeed alone. You must admit that you are not entirely self-sufficient and are dependent on others. There are many ways to reject help, but the most egotistical and sour people have a knack for it, either by refusing the aid or by thanklessly considering it deserved and cutting it off.

To appreciate is to recognize you are not alone in this world and that there are many things of value beyond one's self. We know it's a cliché, but the ability to see the glass as half full is fundamental to good leadership. It comes in handy, for example, following an acquisition. Smucker's has had a history of successful acquisitions, perhaps attributable to this orientation. It values the people and skills it acquires and actively looks for methods, processes, and systems within the acquired company that are superior to its own. Procter & Gamble did much the same when it acquired Gillette. P&G created a special unit to explore and extract the best practices and aspects from each company. As a result, 95 percent of Gillette employees who were invited to stay elected to do so; of those who opted to leave, many did so to take advantage of lucrative change-in-control packages.[19] Each company found value because they looked for it. Sometimes you notice things just by looking.

A few years ago, bona fide good guy Richard Smucker (the current co-CEO of Smucker's and a fourth-generation Smucker) found a letter written by his father that sums up in practical terms what it means to appreciate and express gratitude:

- Say "thank you."

- Listen with full attention.

- Look for the good in others.

- Have a sense of humor.

Thankfulness enables the leaders we interviewed to see the great promise in others, to remain open to experience, and to keep tough situations in perspective without catastrophizing them.

Gratitude is also at the heart of servant-leadership,[20] which might most appropriately be called service-leadership. The premise is that a leader is a steward of a company, with certain responsibilities toward various constituencies, including employees. The corporation exists in a societal context, and one of its purposes is to make a difference in people's lives. That argues for promoting employees' growth in order that they may realize their full potential. There is an obvious business rationale for doing this, but within companies that embrace this philosophy, the goal within servant-leadership is to develop the talents of employees and to build a community in which employees have a mutual interest in personal and corporate improvement and innovation—period. A common definition of leadership is getting results through others. But Robert Price, the reserved former CEO of one of the first modern technology companies (Control Data), reminds us that leadership is "achieving success by making other people successful." That's gratitude for you.

There is more here than meets the eye. How does one feel gratitude or have a sense of appreciation toward those who are being helped? Most observers would say that employees should appreciate their employers for their jobs and for opportunities that may ensue through their jobs. This attitude is apparent when a manager says something like, "Raise? You want a raise? You're lucky to have a job. There are millions of unemployed out there!" Failing to see that he, the manager, is encompassed by the same teleology, he nonetheless conveys who should be beholden to whom.

The key to giving is to give in a way that doesn't create a sense of indebtedness, degrade another's self-respect, or create a chasm that delineates a superior and inferior class. Good leaders achieve this by communicating an attitude. To make the point, let's assume we have two organizations with the same policies that benefit employees. Company A maintains the slogan, "Profiting Through People." The other company, Company B, has the slogan, "Giving Thanks for Enriching Lives," a motto, by the way, that stretches outside of the corporation to include the customer.

In the first instance, the company invests in employees with the clear expectation of a return on its investment. Most companies believe this is entirely reasonable, but the leaders of the organization wouldn't feel particularly appreciative until they got something back. So, the company seems to be saying, "I'm giving you x, y, and z because there is something I want you to do for me." The gift operates as a soft club.

In the second instance, the company's rather offbeat motto seems to say, "It's our privilege to serve, to help people live more fulfilling lives—it's what we do." The point is, the same thing can be given in different ways and accepted or rejected based on the implied terms. And while it's subtle, to be sure, good companies and great leaders appreciate the capabilities and potential in people apart from anything the company might receive from employees in return. The company gives because it is its pleasure and the right thing to do. The fact is, none of the people with whom we spoke for this book consider employees as assets, or capital, or employees for that matter. They consider them as, well, people! Whom would you rather work for? By whom would you rather be led? The entrepreneurial founder of Burt's Bees, Roxanne Quimby, may have said it best when she told us, "It is a compliment when people work for you; I feel very fortunate and thankful for that."

On the other hand, we all have had irritating run-ins with the ungrateful, and it makes you reluctant to ever lift a finger for them again. We think the following joke conveys that emotion. A woman is walking along the beach with her very young son when suddenly a wave rushes in and sweeps the boy out to sea. A passerby, noticing what has happened, runs into the ocean and, after repeated dives, locates the boy on the ocean floor. He manages to pull him to shore where, exhausted, he resuscitates the child to life. He wearily and with great relief looks up at the mother, who says, "He had a hat."[21]

AUTHENTICITY

The concept of authenticity has undergone substantial definitional scrutiny without definitive conclusions being reached. This much has been decided, however: Authenticity in its various guises matters to leadership.[22] It is a valued commodity, both interpersonally and, as manufacturers can attest, in the marketplace, where producers are desperate to apply the label "genuine" to anything from leather goods to fine wines.

What do we mean by authentic and what is it that leaders do that suggest they are more or less authentic? We want to put one understanding of authenticity immediately to rest before moving ahead to address those questions. We are not concerned so much about deep psychological meanings by which people are able to find their true selves, unearthing hidden potential. We certainly hope that all people, leaders included, are able to find within themselves their personal calling and to express themselves accordingly, but such self-actualization is reserved for very few. It's unlikely that every great leader has achieved this level. They're good, but they are not necessarily perfect.

Our view of authenticity and its antonym, fraudulence, is related to what we mean when we say that someone is a poseur. The way in which poseurs present themselves has no correlation to their inner lives and convictions. That is, they don't behave in a way that reflects what they truly think and feel, if these qualities are known to them in the first place. For now, notwithstanding the fact that this disingenuousness may be a blessing for some, since being who they are is precisely the problem, we can ask why anyone would engage in such a ruse.

Jared Sandberg of the *Wall Street Journal* describes just how creepy corporate cloning can get, to the point where employees adopt the same mannerisms, tastes, ideas, and interests as their bosses.[23] One explanation he provides for these behavioral convergences is based on the research of Jennifer Chatman at the Haas School of Business. If you don't know what is required to be successful within a company—an unfortunate but all-too-common scenario—then the closest you might come to doing what appears to matter is to emulate those who are clearly successful. Preliminary attempts to mimic the boss will most likely be selectively rewarded: Boss to employee, "I like the way you think, Jones" (hmm, just like me); boss to employee, "I like the way you dress, Jones" (hmm, just like me); boss to employee, "I like the way you golf, Jones" (hmm, almost as good as me). The point is that it begins with the pairing of two independent events—copying the boss and performance appraisal—then further copying is reinforced by periodic kudos from the boss.

Behaviorists refer to this process as superstitious behavior. You have undoubtedly experienced something similar. Say you are at a soda machine that has just eaten your dollar, and a random kick presumably releases your drink. In fact, a mechanical malfunction delayed its drop and your perfectly timed kick had nothing to do with it. You don't know that, so you're likely to try a well-placed kick the next time something similar occurs. This explanation for conformity is more innocent than those we believe are more operative and less flattering in organizational settings, but it is a worthy rationale backed by solid theory.

Certainly, fearful or ambitiously compliant underlings who are concerned about self-preservation or self-promotion have their reasons to hide their true feelings. That this occurs in organizations is a sad fact of life and is good fodder for corporate lampoonists. But we are interested in why those in leadership positions would not straightforwardly voice their opinions when it seems so natural to do so. We have a couple of explanations.

Mannequin Management

Everyone learns through experience and picks up habits from others. In fact, much of what we do each day requires behavioral repertoires that are similar among people, because the situations we encounter daily call for uniform responses. But management training has raised appropriation to an art. Best practices and case studies—whether intended to support thoughtful inquiry or not—accentuate what has worked in the past and encourage others to follow along. If you want to succeed, do this. Business education breeds formalism. As long as the subject is finance, using equations works just fine, but not so well when the subject is people and human behavior.

Frequently, what students of business learn and never shake free from as they ascend the organizational hierarchy are rules of influence or methods of executing power. To put it delicately, it is the Carnegie-ization of interpersonal behavior; to put it more harshly, it is pure Machiavellianism.[24] Machiavellianism adopts "getting results through others" as the literal definition of leadership. People are viewed as instruments, appendages to the organizational machinery, to be shaped and controlled as any other capital good. If treating people merely as means to ends isn't bad enough, we believe there is something more insidious at work here: Many managers think that's the way it is supposed to be. Our experiences with young graduates suggests that there is little in their education that dissuades them of that idea. If anything, this idea is reinforced by the business press, which repeatedly showcases the executive of the month and invites us all to emulate him or her. There is too little appreciation of the wonderful complexities of individuals and of our magnificent capacity to resist, circumvent, or undermine attempts to control us.

None of our featured leaders, not one, viewed the people who worked for them and the employees of their respective organizations as automatons whose movements could be effectively determined. Instead, they reveled in individuals' intellectual nuances and understood well that this was precisely what they were paying for and that it constituted an important source of competitive advantage.

Playing to the Crowd

We consider deliberate attempts to influence a group strictly through emotional appeals as a type of kitsch-leadership, on a par with photos of kittens on a pillow or painted portraits of children with pleading, oversized eyes. The result is a highly commercialized rendition of leadership. It's sentimental, stylized, and cheap. It's also, again, a counterfeit form of leadership.

Writing about creative expression, Russian novelist Leo Tolstoy uses the word *sincerity* to describe the relationship between the artist and the audience.[25] His description provides an apt metaphor for leadership, since the literal origin of *sincerity* in Russian is "comes from the root." Thus, the demeanor of a leader is the natural and inevitable outgrowth of the interior person who lives within. Conversely, conveying meaning that isn't really one's own will deprive any relationship of genuine intimacy. Jay Ireland learned from his early military experience that leadership necessarily involves developing personal relationships—getting to know the people around you. It is impossible to command effectively without developing a bond with the people whose lives are dependent on the health of the entire group and the decisions the leader ultimately makes.

When leaders such as Bill George, the former CEO of Medtronic and now a successful business writer (author of the aptly named book *Authentic Leadership,* Jossey-Bass, 2003), give authenticity a central place in leadership, they understand what distinguishes genuine leaders from forgers. For illustration, consider what occasionally occurs in the arts. A museum purchases what it thinks is a Vermeer, only to discover many years later that it is the work of the highly proficient Belgian copiest Hans van Meegeran who had perfected Vermeer's technique.[26] In the meantime, paying visitors have shuffled through the museum applauding a work attributed to an artist who died centuries before the current work was actually created. Why take the work down? Why not just say that rather than being an original Vermeer, it's an original van Meegeran? We think the reason is that once we learn the real history of the work, the achievement of van Meegeran decidedly shrinks, and our esteem for Vermeer is reinforced. We admire Vermeer's distinct accomplishments and unique productivity as an artist. If we admire van Meegeran at all, it is not as the progenitor of something novel or uniquely his own, but as a very good forger.

Similarly, all of our leaders, united by kindness, are distinguishable because of their personal styles and special achievements—and these are the things we appreciate. In the words of the serene chairman of Time, Inc., Dick Parsons, " The best person to be as a leader is yourself." Thus, if we have two leaders and we say both are "good," we don't have to provide the same rationale for the claim; we need only to maintain that they are one-of-a-kind people who created something distinctive and worthy of admiration.

This takes us to the next section, on humility. If our leaders weren't accomplished, they wouldn't have anything to be humble about.

HUMILITY

The concept of humility has found its way back into the business lexicon, no doubt partly due to the fine work and observations of academic and author Jim Collins, who recognized its importance to leadership.[27] Its return was long overdue, given what we have had to endure over the past several years: too many corrupt and entitled businesspeople with too little humility.

The value of humility to leadership—and the reason it emerged as such an important asset among our cohort of leaders—owes to the "groundedness" of the people who have it. The "humus" in humility is, quite literally, the dirt beneath their feet. It is what keeps them down-to-earth and gives the organizations they lead special strategic advantages.

Many leaders we spoke with over the years have mentioned humility as an important counterweight to the celebrity CEOs they regarded as seriously flawed and as threats to the longer-term performances of their companies. Without humility to counteract the effects of undue pride, people who seek out the spotlight can behave excessively. They can make a risky and ill-advised acquisition or rashly bet the farm on an unproven product. More specifically, there are several corporate-wide benefits to humility.

Humble Leaders Learn

The Scarecrow in the *Wizard of Oz* (MGM, 1939) astutely notes that, "Some people without brains do an awful lot of talking." The people *with* brains know that if they spend less time talking and more time listening, they might just learn something they didn't know before. Humility facilitates learning, because those who have it recognize that they are not the reservoir of all knowledge and that their success is attributable to many people and factors, including dumb luck.

This aspect of humility seems like a simple skill to master: just shut up for a change and listen. Many executives have attended countless courses and training sessions throughout their careers that ostensibly educate them on how to listen more effectively. But the barriers to listening do not involve deficiencies in skills; adjusting the volume and attention controls does not increase the number of words that register with recipients of messages. That's because the real problem with listening—well or poorly—is psychological in nature.

The psychological hurdle that great artists, scientists, and leaders are able to overcome is the humility hurdle: Knowing that one isn't the sum total of all there is does not imply weakness. Valuing the opinions and expertise of others does not mean that the leader devalues herself. In fact, it is a prerequisite for greatness. Let's face it, Einstein is one of a handful of people whose names will be remembered for many centuries, but he never boasted about his intellectual prowess. Instead, as his memoirs make clear, he was humbled by the mysteries of the universe and readily acknowledged his own limitations in his pursuits.[28]

In contrast, we have both met our fair share of "bubble boys" who go to great lengths to protect a self-image of invulnerability and superiority, which distances them from precisely what they wish to excel at: leadership. But just ask them—they think they are pretty good at it. They are successful autocrats, but poor learners. As a consequence, they and their companies are incapable of adapting.

The problems with leaders who lack humility run much deeper than a simple inability to listen, since such leaders are unable to hear in a number of ways—all of which are psychologically designed to preserve a glowing, but fragile, self-concept. As positive and negative information comes to them, here is what they do with it:

- Take credit for the success.

- Smile approvingly at those who congratulate them for success.

- Blame others or unfavorable circumstances for failure.

- Aggress against those who suggest something might be wrong with the company and that there is a need to change.

With this outlook, in short order a leader will hear only what he wants to hear and will be surrounded only by those who are wont to "stay positive."

Humble leaders aren't frightened by the truth and go to great lengths to ensure that they receive it. The strategic advantage of getting at the truth is self-evident. The added benefit, however, is that people who have felt free to voice their opinions and to advance their truths know they have been heard and are more likely to accept the outcomes of decisions, even if the decisions may not be entirely to their liking. Rick Levin, the renowned economist and president of Yale University, has to deal with multiple constituencies when promoting the overall welfare of the university. He has been able to move the university forward first and foremost by listening to everyone who has an interest in the future of Yale and then crafting a direction that appeals to all stakeholders—or at least that doesn't sacrifice one interest for the sake of another.

In some instances, as in the case of Yale, a leader must first prove that he is listening by establishing goals that expressly put the organization in harmony with particular constituencies. When Rick Levin took over as president of Yale, one of his first goals was to improve the town-gown relations, which had gradually deteriorated prior to his tenure. To restore the trust of the community in the intentions of Yale, Levin made the relationship with New Haven a priority throughout the organization. For example, Yale created an innovative and lucrative subsidy program that promotes home ownership and attracts purchasers to New Haven, and has invested heavily in the city's retail market and economic development. Today, the relationship he rebuilt continues to thrive.

Humble Leaders Are Realistic

Humility exists midway between unjustified low self-regard and excessive self-regard. Said differently, humble leaders keep things in perspective. This is a very good thing, since there is a significant allure to being able to contort perspective as nimbly as a Chinese acrobat.

Humble leaders demonstrate two sides of realism. First, they temper their optimism with astute and honest assessments of corporate capability. They are pragmatists who understand what the organization is able to do and how quickly it can move. A surfeit of optimism has been found to be a potentially adverse bias in all of us, but for those who are far less than humble, it may spell particular trouble: An exuberant assuredness of success built on hasty preparation is unlikely to yield the promised results—and will likely end in disaster.[29]

Indeed, overconfidence combined with public pronouncements about a glorious future may make the second component of realism harder to satisfy. The second side to realism is recognizing when the direction the company (or business unit, product line, etc.) is heading is no longer viable and ending the mission. In general, a willingness to disengage from a losing course of action is very difficult, resulting from faulty cognitions to which we all are susceptible.[30] One name given to this phenomenon is the Concorde Effect, after the now-defunct supersonic jet. As building commenced, it became increasingly evident that the jet would never be profitable, and yet construction was completed and it was put into service.[31] There is a panoply of explanations for the Concorde Effect, but regardless of which explanation is most accurate, clearly self-deception and delusions about the true state of affairs will not help. And so, those who guard their personas and are threatened by being incorrect will persist in a faltering course of action even though the evidence weighs against them.

There is one more important ancillary note to realism involving the critical role of spouses. We have been fortunate enough to get to know several of the family members of the leaders in our sample. Their spouses are loving and supportive, but they are by no means enamored of or vicariously captivated by status, money, and power. Unimpressed, they rolled their eyes in mock opposition and firmly expressed their own ideas, some of which ran counter to the opinions of our leaders, and some helpfully reconstructed our leaders' faulty memories. If there is any Olympian attraction to high places, spouses are the people who grab onto leaders and yank them back down to earth. We cannot say enough about the power of spouses in the lives of our leaders. They are naturally central to family dynamics, but, less obviously, they function as touchstones for reality.

Humble Leaders Are Charitable, Not Self-Centered

Certain moments and encounters, no matter how casual or fleeting, make an immediate impact. Why the following brief incident became a defining moment in a decades-long quest to understand human behavior in organizations is hard to say, except that it simply and elegantly demonstrated the opposite of humility: narcissism (humility has been found to be negatively correlated with what is known as the Dark Triad—Psychopathy, Machiavellianism, and Narcissism).[32] Narcissus, the young huntsman in Ovid's story, gazed admiringly at his own reflection in a pool of water and became the namesake for the personality disorder (see the *Diagnostic and Statistical Manual of Mental Disorders,* published by the American Psychiatric Association). Narcissists are preoccupied with their self-importance, power, brilliance, and uniqueness and expect others to unquestionably adhere to their expectations—and consequently tend to surround themselves with people who are more than happy to comply. They are not charitable people.

Once upon a time, O'Malley was an internal consultant for a major company conducting weeklong management seminars as a part of his job. These were programs conducted on-site within the corporate learning center. Often, company executives simultaneously would hold meetings at the center, and refreshments and foods would be available to them. The participants in the programs—including instructors—were asked to refrain from circling the concessionaires and eating their food.

On one occasion, O'Malley asked the senior vice president of Human Resources of the sponsor company to drop by his class to give a lecture. Before the class, the executive offered O'Malley a soda and food from one of the executive meetings taking place. O'Malley diplomatically mentioned that there was a company policy that prohibited the pilfering of food from others' meetings. The senior vice president helped himself anyway. Now, we are no goody-two-shoes, but what strikes us most from this simple vignette is the ease with which he disregarded the corporate policy and proceeded to break a rule that—it seems to us, in retrospect—he didn't see as relevant to him. And he was willing to waive the rule for others as well. To complete the picture, this same executive later was asked to leave the company for breaking other, far more important rules. It appears that the inclination to "just help yourself" was a foundational aspect of his personality.

He had achieved great success, and he certainly wasn't the malignant narcissist fiend Patrick Bateman—who lives a soulless Wall Street dream by day and kills by night—from *American Psycho* (Universal Studios, 2000). But he did possess a self-important entitlement and insist upon the preferential attention of a functioning narcissist, and therein lies the rub. He mistook the elevated status of his position as personal worthiness—a concept that is completely foreign to the leaders in our sample. What does anyone's position have to do with who they are?

THE HUMOR ADVANTAGE

Recently, I (O'Malley) went hiking in the Adirondacks with my family, a hike that was described as easy in the guidebook we were using but was tortuous for my wife and me. The kids had no problem.

Fatigued on our descent, my wife tripped on an exposed root and commenced a lengthy, slow-motion stumble that culminated in an unladylike sprawl on the ground. I was a helpless spectator to it all. Once I learned that she had escaped only with a mild abrasion on her hand, I did what any caring husband would do: I laughed. Oh, come on, it's funny! But why?

Philosopher Henri Bergson proposed that such falls were physical manifestations of mechanical, inelastic lives.[33] That is, the body failed us; it needed to be less rigid, better attuned to the surroundings, and more adaptive. Laughter is the reminder that our lives are supposed to be more pliable, playful, and creative versus weighted down by social gravitas and relentlessly burdened by the presumed seriousness of everything.

Among other things, humor is a wake-up call to lighten up and view problems in a different light. And there is much to recommend for humor: A sense of humor has been related to interpersonal competencies such as warmth, ability to listen, flexible thinking and perspective-taking, openness, maturity, and kindness.[34] It is no wonder, then, that the leaders with whom we spoke included humor on their list of essentials for kind leadership.

That's not to say humor cannot be abused. Baker once worked at a television station whose culture was to use "humor" to make fun of or unsettle employees, believing that these actions fostered a creative environment. The boss would often come to work and say, "Today I'll be working on 'the Smith problem'," when talking to employee Smith. The Christmas parties were particularly horrific; when key managers had too much libation, they mocked other managers using so-called humor. It was a very poisonous environment.

On the other hand, one of the best managers we've ever met, Jim Tisch, chairman of Loews Corporation, always ends his letters and e-mails with wonderful, complimentary, playful closes reflecting the content of the subject matter. Examples are: for letters of recommendation—Enthusiastically yours; for annual fund solicitation letters—Annually yours; for a letter containing a check payable to the American Skin Association benefit—Epidermally yours; a thank-you note to a sponsor of "New York Goes to War"—Bellicosely yours; a letter containing a check for an organization whose motto is "Keep the fires burning"—Flammably yours. He's known for that loving and respectful humor that fosters an air of collegiality and friendship, even during the most difficult times.

Another leader we have seen in action would often preface very challenging meetings by saying, "I wish my mother was here to help," or "Maybe we should start this one with a prayer"—an abbreviated, lighthearted way to convey that difficulties lay ahead. Humor and openness reflect a person who is approachable and collaborative. And there are other benefits too, as described below.

Anxiety Management

As demonstrated by the episode of the falling wife, humor and laughter are natural reactions to stress. They express relief. Knowing that the fallen wife was all right gave her husband permission to laugh.

Humor also diminishes the anxieties associated with stressors. Cracking a well-timed joke can put people at ease and give them a sense of control over the situation. The use of humor is an assertion that one is unafraid and will not allow oneself to be overwhelmed by events. Writers sometimes help us out by using comic relief as a literary device. Humor is used as a momentary distraction from disturbing, painful experiences: thus, the gravediggers in *Hamlet* and the gardeners in *Richard II*. We have often thought that executives could use something akin to court jesters to occasionally refocus their attention toward what matters most.

The famous and well-established Yerkes-Dodson law proposes that people are unable to perform well when anxieties are too high (or too low): There is too much emotional interference to allow peak performance. Humor can be an effective mediator between emotion and performance.

Good leaders such as Richard Smucker use humor effectively to manage anxieties, and that, in our opinion, is one of the most fundamental roles of leadership. The J.M. Smucker Company helps employees moderate anxiety in another way as well. It has a room called Cassin-Young where employees can go to reflect—a "thinking spot." The room is named after the destroyer Smucker's father fought on while stationed in the Pacific during World War II. The room is a reminder that no matter how dismal the situation may appear, it could always be worse. Whether or not people actually use the room is immaterial, since the room itself symbolizes a state of mind.

Group Cohesion

"What's round and purple and commutes to work? An Abelian grape."[35] We'll pause to give you time to look up *Abelian* in the dictionary in order to get the joke.

Although we didn't laugh at this joke either, because we don't have the mathematical backgrounds to understand it, we can imagine group theorists at a mathematics conference laughing their heads off. The point is that many jokes are what Ted Cohen of the University of Chicago Philosophy Department has called *hermetic*. They are sealed, except to a select group that has sufficient knowledge and background to appreciate the humor. Some audiences will get it, and some audiences will not. Some people are insiders, and some people are outsiders, but in the context of companies, humor serves a healthy purpose of bringing people together. Using humor to scoff at a competitor, to question a silly operating procedure, or to ridicule some harmless organizational folly allows people to forge connections. It is humor meant for the community that only the community can understand.

Humor also encourages organizational members to join the organizational community. We might say that humor socializes. If you want to get in on future jokes, you had better learn the language and nuances of the company. If you are a newcomer who does not want to remain the target of jokes, learn fast.

It's hard for outsiders to be humorous inside of companies, particularly when the setting bleeds "seriousness." During a board meeting of a major supermarket chain just before Thanksgiving, one of the executive members of the board was describing the company's point system, by which customers could earn a free turkey when a certain amount of purchases was converted into points. The executive proceeded: "One hundred points and you get a ten-pound turkey; two hundred points and you get a fifteen-pound turkey; three hundred points and you get a twenty-pound turkey." One of us continued the progression: "Wow! I'd love to see the size of turkey you'd get at a thousand points." Total silence. Oh, come on, it's funny!

NOTES

1. McCoy, B. (2007). Success. *Vital Speeches of the Day*, July: 321–322.

2. As cited in Purcell, R.C., Jr. (1988). Values for value: Integrating and stewardship. *Vital Speeches of the Day*, 64: 763–766.

3. Weber, M., & Eisenstadt, S.N. (1968). *Max Weber on Charisma and Institution Building*. Chicago: University of Chicago Press.

4. For representative readings on charisma, see Conger, J.A., & Kanungo, R.N. (1987). Toward a behavioral theory of charismatic leadership in organizational settings. *Academy of Management Review*, 12: 637–647; House, R.J., & Howell, J.M. (1992). Personality and charismatic leadership. *Leadership Quarterly*, 3: 81–108.

5. Nussbaum, M. (1996). Compassion: The basic social emotion. *Social Philosophy and Policy*, 13: 27–58.

6. The following example is borrowed from Frost, P.J. (1999). Why compassion counts! *Journal of Management Inquiry*, 8: 127–133.

7. For a representative set of readings on emotional intelligence, see Conte, J.M. (2005). A review and critique of emotional intelligence measures. *Journal of Organizational Behavior*, 26: 433–440; Goleman, D. (1995). *Emotional Intelligence: Why It Can Matter More than IQ*. New York: Bantam; Mayer, J.D., & Salovey, P. (1993). The intelligence of emotional intelligence. *Intelligence*, 17: 433–442; Mayer, J.D., Salovey, P., & Caruso, D.R. (2004). Emotional intelligence: Theory, findings and implications. *Psychological Inquiry*, 15: 197–215; Zeidner, M., Matthew, G., & Roberts, R.D. (2004). Emotional intelligence in the workplace: A critical review. *Applied Psychology: An International Review*, 53: 371–399.

8. Trevino, L.K., Hartman, L.P., and Brown, M. (2000). Moral person and moral manager: How executives develop a reputation for ethical leadership. *California Management Review*, 42: 128–142.

9. As reported in Koehn, D. (2005). Integrity as a business asset. *Journal of Business Ethics*, 58: 125–136.

10. The analogy of a bridge is taken from Dudzinski, D.M. (2004). Integrity: Principled coherence, virtue or both. *Journal of Value Inquiry*, 38: 299–313.

11. Guth, R.A. (2007). Inside Microsoft's plan to bring in outside talent. *Wall Street Journal*, September 26: B1.

12. Heineman, B.W. (2007). Avoiding integrity land mines. *Harvard Business Review*, April: 100–108.

13. Kouzes, J.M., & Posner, B.Z. (2005). Leading in cynical times. *Journal of Management Inquiry*, 14: 357–364.

14. For a thorough review of source credibility, see Pornpitak-pan, C. (2004). The persuasiveness of source credibility: A critical review of five decades' evidence. *Journal of Applied Social Psychology*, 34: 243–281.

15. Nocera, J. (2008). "Put Buyers First? What a Concept." *New York Times*, January 5: C1.

16. Abshire, D. (2006). Trust and General Hal Moore. *Vital Speeches of the Day*, August: 581–583.

17. This gem was passed along to us by Randy Barnett, a professor at Georgetown University Law School; it originated with his grandfather.

18. A number of articles informed discussion throughout this section: Emmons, R.A., & McCullough, M.E. (2003). Counting blessings versus burdens: An experimental investigation of gratitude and subjective well-being in daily life. *Journal of Personality and Social Psychology*, 84: 377–389; Fitzgerald, P. (1998). Gratitude and justice. *Ethics*, 109: 119–153; Watkins, P.C., Woodward, K., Stone, T., & Kolts, R.L. (2003). Gratitude and happiness: Development of a measure of gratitude, and relationships with subjective well-being. *Social Behavior and Personality*, 31: 431–452.

19. Briefing: Procter & Gamble (2007). *Economist*, August 11: 61.

20. The idea of servant-leadership was introduced by Greenleaf; see, for example, Greenleaf, R.K. (1977). *Servant-Leadership: A Journey Into the Nature of Legitimate Power and Greatness*. NY: Paulist Press; Greenleaf, R.K. (1996). *On Becoming a Servant Leader*. San Francisco: Jossey-Bass.

21. This joke comes from: Sangoff, M. (1985). Criticism and countertheses: "He had a hat." *Journal of Aesthetics and Art Criticism*, 44: 191–192.

22. For a recent overview of authentic leadership, see Avolio, B.J., & Gardner, W.L. (2005). *Leadership Quarterly*, 16: 315–338,

23. Sandberg, J. (2007). The Stepford staff: Or how it happens that a boss is cloned. *Wall Street Journal*, July 24: B1.

24. By Carnegie-ization, we mean a practiced, insincere approach to winning friends and influencing people. By Machiavellianism, we mean the detached, calculating person who will go to great lengths—including the use of deception—to get what he or she wants.

25. Tolstoy, L. (2001). *What Is Art?* Trans. Aylmer Maude. Bridgewater, NJ: Replica Books.

26. This example, and the reasons quality forgeries don't merit the same esteem as originals, is found in Dutton, D. (1979). Artistic crimes. The problem of forgery in the arts. *British Journal of Aesthetics*, 19: 302–341.

27. Collins, J. (2001). *Good to Great*. New York: Harper Business.

28. Dukas, H. and Hoffman, B., eds. (1979), *Albert Einstein, The Human Side: New Glimpses from His Archives.* Princeton, NJ: Princeton University Press.

29. Lovallo, D, & Kahneman, D. (2003). Delusions of success: How optimism undermines executives' decisions. *Harvard Business Review*, July: 56–63.

30. Brockner, J. (1992). The escalation of commitment to a failing course of action: Toward theoretical progress. *Academy of Management Review*, 17: 39–61.

31. Arkes, H.R., & Ayton, P. (1999). The sunk cost and Concorde effects: Are humans less rational than lower animals? *Psychological Bulletin*, 125: 591–600.

32. Lee, K., & Ashton, M.C. (2005). Psychopathy, Machiavellianism and narcissism in the five-factor model and the HEXACO model of personality structure. *Personality and Individual Differences*, 38: 1571–1582.

33. Bergson, H. (1917). *Laughter: An Essay on the Meaning of the Comic*. Trans. C. Brereton and F. Rothwell. New York: Macmillan.

34. Richman, J. (2001). Humor and creative life styles. *American Journal of Psychotherapy*, 55: 420–428; Yip, J.A., & Martin, R.A. (2006). Sense of humor, emotional intelligence, and social competence. *Journal of Research in Personality*, 40: 1202–1208.

35. Cohen, T. (1999). High and low art, and high and low audiences. *Journal of Aesthetics and Art Criticism*, 57: 137–143.

EXPECTATIONS MATTER

A recent research study estimated that only 63 percent of the financial performance promised by strategy is delivered.[1] Like heat escaping from the crevices of homes, the remaining 37 percent of performance seeps out of the system and vanishes into thin air. The majority of the reasons for this loss—about 30 percent—relate to poor communications and organizational structures that impede execution. The specific factors that impair performance echo those voiced by Michael Cherkasky. His three-part recipe for capturing performance potential is based on three constituent ingredients: clarity, accountability, and consequences.

THE GREAT GULF

Hurricane Katrina seemed to have taken everyone by surprise. Along with its path of destruction, the hurricane left bewilderment on the faces of federal and local officials, whose pathetic response is now a part of American lore. In truth, the potential dangers of a hurricane entering the gulf at just the right angle were well publicized for decades. Why, the Federal Emergency Management Agency (FEMA) even held a five-day trial exercise in Louisiana the year prior to Katrina, code-named "Hurricane Pam." The goal was to develop an integrated regional response to a catastrophic surge in water levels, and the distinguished New Orleans paper, the *Times-Picayune*, wrote about the possible effects of "Pam" in a series. Despite the preparations, however, when the real thing hit, the official reaction was inefficient and disorderly: when the organization had to put its training to use by mobilizing a set of meaningful, coherent actions. There comes a time for every organization when knowing what to do just isn't enough. Collectively, the three-part prescription above is intended to overcome an inertia that exists in many organizations, where general knowledge of facts and circumstances rarely leads to effective responses. Philosopher John Gibson offers an apt description that highlights the gulf between awareness and action, and the failure to react to the demands that circumstances place upon us:[2]

> . . . let us imagine a person I will call the Simpleton. The Simpleton, we will agree, is a sort of *mere* knower. He looks at a wounded person and rightly says 'You are in pain.' But the Simpleton 'behaves' with his knowledge in such a way that we find a certain vacancy in his grasp of what it is that he is saying. I ask him whether he thinks your inquiry is serious, to which he offers an earnest 'yes.' But he offers his 'yes' without any gesture that hints that by this 'yes' he understands what *he* is thereby called on to do. As I begin tending to you, I yell to him that he ought to call for an ambulance. He nods in sincere agreement and then falls still. And when I tell the Simpleton that you might not recover without his assistance, he responds with an honest 'That's right' and then lapses back into inactivity. . . . In this sense we see that his knowledge is idle, lifeless, for his mind goes dead precisely when it ought

to become animated. In a word, he is an idiot who just happens to know as much as we do, an eerie sort of idiot savant.

The questions before us in this chapter are, "How do we get someone who has basic intellectual aptitude and a healthy reservoir of knowledge to take necessary actions and perform well? How do we prevent him from becoming a lost cause or simply that person who never lived up to his or her potential?"

CLARITY

Clarity exists at different organizational levels. At the macro level, it involves articulating meaning and vision for the company, its value system, and its strategic pathways. At the micro level, it involves framing communications that elicit action and defining specific goals in the service of the company's overall mission. We will discuss each of these in the successive subsections, starting with dimensions that define the bigger picture.

Making Meaning

Antoine de Saint-Exupéry admonished, "If you want to build a ship, don't drum up the [crew] to gather wood, divide the work, and give orders. Instead, teach them to yearn for the vast and endless sea."[3] Companies that have a sense of higher purpose attract and retain passionate employees. Procter & Gamble, Smucker's, Rodale, Vanguard, and Tupperware all have it. They don't just sell detergents, jellies, magazines, financial security, or products; they make life easier, bring families together, help to make people more secure, and so forth.

Beyond the day-to-day concerns about market shares and profits, these companies are all trying to improve the world and peoples' lives. That may sound idealistic, but that's what these leaders are: idealists. They are doing their best for society in their own ways.

Indeed, the quest for a better world has to supply much of the inspiration, lest one give up in despair. Vanguard founder Jack Bogle relates the following story, as told to him by Reverend Fred Craddock of Georgia.[4] The reverend, visiting the home of a niece, strikes up a conversation with an old greyhound dog that once raced at the local track and had been taken in by the niece.

> I said to the dog, 'Are you still racing?' 'No,' he replied. 'Well, what was the matter? Did you get too old to race?' 'No, I still have some race in me.' 'Well, what then? Did you not win?' 'I won over a million dollars for my owner.' 'Well, what was it? Bad treatment?' 'Oh, no,' the dog said, 'they treated us royally when we were racing.' 'Did you get crippled?' 'No.' 'Then why?' Craddock pressed, 'Why?' The dog answered, 'I quit.' 'You quit?' 'Yes,' he said, 'I quit.' 'Why did you quit?' 'I just *quit*. Because after all that running and running and running, I found out that the rabbit I was chasing wasn't even real.'

Regardless of whether good leaders believe in a meaning *of* life, all of our leaders believe in a meaning *in* life and wish that for others. Uninspired and more conventional executives see the work to be done as filling boxes, slapping labels on bottles, or painting machinery. Great leaders don't want this limited perspective for themselves or others.

"The moon has no light of its own." These words, spoken by the motivational chairman and CEO of John Deere & Company, Robert

Lane, distinguish between a reflective surface and the source of the light. To John Deere, measures of economic profit are indirect indicators of whose glow is dimmer or brighter in relation to the real energy source: serving and satisfying customers while very carefully managing assets, leveraging efficient processes, and developing talent. When balanced attention is paid to these multiple factors, healthy financial results are reflected on the income statement and balance sheet.

When we attend a Broadway show, we marvel at the energy and professionalism of the players and wonder how they can perform in the same play or musical two or three times a day for several days a week. Some shows last many years. Employees are also asked to perform with similar regularity and consistency, and we can legitimately wonder how they are able to do it as well. Our reflexive reply to the latter is, "They don't."

That is, they don't unless they have a place worth going to and a job worth doing. Actors and actresses have their off nights, but by and large they wouldn't be able to function at their level of proficiency without passion, one of CEO Maria Rodale's (of Rodale Publishing) Three Ps for leadership success: Passion, Persistence, and Patience. Broadway performers don't show up at work to see how prettily they can sing a song: They show up to entertain an audience and to make its members glad they came. In addition, performers don't show up as people who dance or sing, they arrive as dancers and singers. The point is that passion distinguishes the identities of those who are serious about their craft from mere hobbyists or wishful thinkers.[5]

In addition, the setting where professionals perform has an effect on their psyche. Imagine the ornate theaters where some of the greatest artists have taken the stage, and the enthusiastic crowd gathered to greet them. The scene of the performance has much to do with the performance itself, because it signals that something special, something exciting, is about to occur.

During antiquity, the concept of a scene referred to a place where something stood apart from the typical and where something more vivid and animated was anticipated to occur: a stage, a tent, a tabernacle, or some other distinct forum that demarcated the ordinary from the profound. Thus, today, making "the scene" is to go where the action is.[6] Often "scenes" are places that encourage participation, architectural locations that require some form of appreciative behavior if these places are to fulfill their functions.[7] Elegant boardrooms and palatial theaters evoke certain reactions in visitors and subtly prompt them to observe decorum. If the place is to come alive and properly facilitate the action that will occur there, people must do what is expected of them.

Unfortunately, office buildings and office stalls just don't evoke the same kind of vigor found in the great performance halls, nor the momentousness found in the great synagogues and cathedrals. There is nothing special about most places of business, but there are notable exceptions. The campus of the household goods company S.C. Johnson contains three Frank Lloyd Wright buildings. One employee's comments echo the general sentiment of working in a masterpiece.[8] "Working here is amazing. People feel as if they're coming into a cathedral. It's inspirational. Staff and visitors have an emotional reaction to buildings like these." Companies won't want to drain the corporate coffers to create architectural masterpieces, but a little thought devoted to what distinguishes the place of work from the mundane world outside can go a very long way.

Values

"A great song has both great lyrics *and* great music," says Pete Peterson, the socially conscious senior chairman of the Blackstone Group, referring to the way companies often give lip service to the social glue of their institutions, their core values. They get the lyrics right—the posters with words on them—but forget that a meaningful musical score entails much more.

To appreciate the difficulty of implementing a value system that works, let's consider an example. There are different types of values. There are those that govern personal conduct in general, such as integrity and respect. And there are those that attempt to orient people toward a certain aspect of the business, such as innovation, quality, or customer service. For our example, let's look at the latter and assess what goes into giving the following company credo motivational force:

> "We are a customer-focused company dedicated to providing superior customer service."

Nice words. Many companies utter them, but not all companies pursue their implications with the same conviction. In order to change employees' behaviors toward customers, the company must first:

- Change employee attitudes toward the customer, and

- Create group norms that reinforce those attitudes

An attitude consists of *beliefs* about customers and an *evaluation* of the importance of those beliefs—beliefs are the factual components of attitudes, and evaluations are renderings of personal relevance and meaning toward those beliefs. *Norms* are beliefs and attitudes that have been systemically adopted.[9]

A decrement in any component results in a reduced likelihood of action. For example, we can believe that the sky is falling, but not care and so do nothing to get out of the way. Or we might care, but notice that no one else seems to share our belief or our concern, and so, again, do nothing. To return to Pete Peterson's observation, it isn't so easy to affect behavior change because there is quite a lot that has to be aligned before people budge.

Consider the complications that our customer can cause. The company maintains that a laserlike focus on the customer is the key to success, and the leader repetitiously conveys this through every communication to employees. Yet, this hypothetical company has no reliable means of staying in touch with customers and tapping into what is important to them, and the company is structured around its regions through local profit and loss centers: A customer that spans a given region will have a hard time getting unified service. This company is unlikely to obtain service-promoting behaviors from the rank and file even if employees individually believe the customer can add value to the company. They will think that in the scheme of things, customer service isn't important enough to warrant a fundamental change in their outlook.

Now suppose the top executive reorganizes the company around customers and creates new mechanisms for capturing the needs and feedback of customers. Further, the CEO initiates customer studies, personally visiting every major customer, that take him away from home for half the days of the year. In addition, metrics that assess various aspects of customer satisfaction are introduced, and employee recognition and reward are partially based on those measures.

Suddenly, the norms of the organization begin to shift. A more uniform belief system that is increasingly appreciative of customers begins to emerge—before, customers ironically were perceived as nuisances that got in the way of profitability. Employees now admit to believing that the company is indeed customer-focused, and there is a growing cross-company consistency in that belief. But something still isn't quite right.

The CEO expected a much more enthusiastic response from employees and more encouraging behavior change at the executive level. He has observed some progress, but it is lagging, and employee responses remain half-hearted. It seems that some people in key positions have not adopted the changes and that "serving the customer" is perceived negatively. That is, their attitude toward the company's new initiative is that it is an imposition. The new structure has stripped them of their regional fiefdoms and power, changing the way that they must operate and requiring a slightly different work regimen and moderately more travel. Some people have to do things entirely differently, and some are poorly equipped to do so. Some middle managers who formerly spent hours in their offices compiling numbers for the P&L and monitoring costs feel lost.

The CEO, sensing the resistance and hearing rumbles within the leadership group intimating that they are prepared to wait out the changes, that "this too shall pass," meets with his top team. The CEO knows that he can't change the company on his own and that he needs to leverage the talents of leaders throughout the organization. It becomes clear that some leaders within the ranks will be unable to comply with the new demands of the organization, and they are asked to step aside: As Tupperware CEO Rick Goings says, "Lead, follow, or get out of the way." Soon, those with a service mentality, free of competing vested interests, occupy key positions in the company and appraise the direction of the company favorably. To put the icing on the cake, the company begins to see the new customer focus pay off for the business in the form of new products and services and greater revenues and profits. The new customer-based value system takes hold.

This has been a long story, we know. But changing a value system is a lengthy process, and we hope we have related the inherent difficulties. Simple words are not enough. We recently had people over to our house, and one of the guests mentioned the research of a friend of his who was investigating whether facts lead to behavior change. One of us spontaneously, and we suppose rudely, laughed at the thesis. Facts, shmacts. Facts don't move people unless the people and those around them care about the facts.

And this brings us to an executive's ability to really change the culture of a mature organization. There's a great deal of debate on this subject. Some believe a company's culture is so ingrained in the operation that it cannot be changed without replacing the top tier of management. Others believe change can be achieved with clear directives from the top. All agree it is extremely difficult.

Bill was managing a large national business and made a valiant attempt to change the culture of the company from a tough, ossified, top-down approach to a more collegial one. And it happened. The first adjustment made was to stop moving managers around arbitrarily just for the sake of change. While there were some positives in getting new ideas and approaches from new unit heads, the effort necessary for the staff to adjust to new managers every couple of years was so traumatic it kept the business units from maximizing output. Through discontinuing the movement of managers, keeping them situated, and holding them accountable, units became much more productive. The bottom line showed it. More importantly, the employees felt better about their workplace because they knew what to expect from a manager whom they got to really know.

On another occasion, as president of a different company, Baker attempted to change the culture of a well-known and respected institution by making it less bureaucratic and more flexible. Try as he might (short of a wholesale management replacement), he just couldn't make it happen. The place was already very successful, so Baker decided to live with a little bureaucracy and maximize the other great strengths of the organization. This time the culture changed the president, not the other way around.

Focus and Frames

Very often, it isn't what you say that matters, but how you say it. The best leaders have a knack for saying the right things in the right ways.

Those ways help to structure, or frame, meanings and thoughts. They are mental windows through which we perceive and understand possible scenarios in particular ways.[10] Presenting the invasion of Iraq as part of a larger "war on terror," for example, is one such construction that promotes a particular outlook on reality and constrains problem definitions, interpretations, evaluations, and treatments to that perspective. We are asked to evaluate our assault on terrorism through the lens of "war," and that implies certain responses, but not others.

The paradigmatic example of a message frame comes from the widely cited experiment by Amos Tversky and Daniel Kahneman.[11] You are asked to imagine the outbreak of an unusual disease that is expected to kill 600 people in the absence of any intervention. In the first scenario, you are presented with two programs and asked which course of action you would take, A or B.

A. If Program A is adopted, 200 people will be saved.

B. If Program B is adopted, there is a one-third probability that 600 people will be saved, and a two-thirds probability that no people will be saved.

Which option would you choose?

Now consider a second scenario that presents you with another pair of choices.

A. If Program A is adopted, 400 people will die.

B. If Program B is adopted, there is a one-third probability that nobody will die, and a two-thirds probability that 600 people will die.

Again, which would you choose?

The programmatic choices in the two scenarios are equivalent, but in the first scenario, the decision is framed in terms of lives saved

(Tversky and Kahneman would say "gains"), and in the second scenario the decision is framed in terms of lives lost ("losses"). If you are
like most people, however, despite the logical equivalence of the
choices, you selected "A" in scenario one and "B" in scenario two.
When problems are presented as something to be gained, people tend
to be risk-averse: They prefer the sure bet. Conversely, when problems
are presented as something to be lost, people are risk-seeking: They
are willing to take a chance in order to obtain a more favorable outcome than the given alternatives would produce.

Suppose you are the head of marketing and you would like to introduce a new soda, drug, or cosmetic that potentially would appeal
to customers who already buy a similar product of yours (think diet
versus a regular beverage). You can stay put in anticipation of the predictable revenue stream from your current product, or chance a new
product introduction that can either augment or dilute existing sales.
If you want the organization to devote resources to the new product,
you will have to ask it to take a risk, and the way to ask will be to
frame the request in terms of what might be lost if the new product
isn't developed.

> If we don't add complementary products to our line, our sin-
> gle product will be vulnerable to competitors, and there is a
> significant chance we will lose market share in the near future.
> Our best hope of checking decline is to add another product
> that builds greater brand awareness and thwarts the dismal
> prospect of a nongrowth future.

In addition to making positive or negative portrayals of the same
information, it also is possible to place emphasis on certain dimensions
of an issue or problem by situating it in a certain light. The practice
of preferential hiring, for example, can be presented as affirmative
action, reverse discrimination, or equal opportunity. Each depiction

highlights certain aspects over others that will appeal more or less to various audiences. Affirmative action makes historical racial bias salient; reverse discrimination raises awareness of relative merit; equal opportunity draws attention to access to quality education and initial inequalities.

Andy Stern, the visionary head of the 1.9-million-member Service Employees International Union, underscores the importance of reframing the conversation, especially one that has grown tired and outdated. The way you say something makes people more or less receptive. The old conversation, the old frame, is that unions are anti-capitalist, anti-business, anti-company, and anti-trade—a conversation that not many wish to listen to because, first, it is far removed from new global realities and the nature of competition, and, second, the win-lose orientation invites self-inflicted harms. The conversation Stern envisions is one that he aptly calls "Team America": a united country engaged in a mission of improving lives, where businesses can flourish and provide meaningful, rewarding work. It is the language of *partnership* versus *conflict*.

Similarly, any negotiation can be differentially pitched either as a problem to be mutually solved or as a dilemma in which one person must win and the other lose. Michael Critelli presented analogous choices at Pitney Bowes by affecting the comparison for corporate success. In looking at traditional competitors, the company's market share was impressive. But he asked Pitney Bowes to think in terms of its percent participation in worldwide mail services, and here the contrast wasn't as favorable—suggesting that there was much work to be done.

Goal Setting

Regardless of your level in the organization, there is generally some attempt to set goals. At times these attempts can be feeble, but usually

the value of having goals, regardless of how poorly they may be artic-
ulated and monitored, is recognized. We don't believe any research
supports the idea of exhorting employees to do their best without having tangible goals in place to shape their direction.

We realize that the value of goals is well established in organizations and that we need not say much more about them, other than to
make a few miscellaneous comments.[12]

- It doesn't make sense to hold someone accountable,
  through reward or punishment, for objectives that are
  ill defined or poorly communicated.

- Important goals to which people are committed have
  motivational force. That is, other than performing a di-
  rective function, stretch goals have the complementary
  advantage of energizing people to persistently work
  toward something they want to achieve.

- Setting goals is often mistaken as the end in itself.
  Think about it. We have all established goals, believed
  they were important, and done nothing to meet them.
  That is because each day our goals compete with other
  distractions and priorities. It is easy to set goals and
  much harder for us to clear the way to attain them. That
  is where leadership and kindly reminders of what is
  most important and what must get done come in handy.

- Set goals in the context of *thinking big*. If there is a
  mantra of our leadership group, it is the one succinctly
  voiced by John Pepper: "Go for the big win." Too often,
  goals are grounded in the customary ways of doing
  things in the industry—and there is little sense
  in expending substantial energy swatting flies. Some
  companies that find themselves in a comfortable niche

are happy with the status quo; some big companies believe they can't afford to change—they have too much invested in the way things are and are pleased with the current state of affairs. But employees don't like to be associated with mediocrity. Leaders who have grander ambitions and ask for more from the workforce are inviting employees to participate in a bigger story than the one to which they are accustomed: That's not a bad invitation!

- Make certain that individual goals do not impair group performance. Most companies temper the potentially detrimental effects of personal pursuits by giving greater weight to group goals in compensation plans.

- Avoid the trap of setting long-term goals without specifying intermediate subgoals, celebrating improvements, or making effort secondarily reinforcing (we do the latter, for example, when we treat ourselves to a warm fire or special coffee while writing).

- Don't lose sight of the many accomplishments that occur outside of the formal goal-setting process. It is impossible to identify everything that will need to be done in advance of a fiscal year; therefore, it is essential to recognize meritorious achievements that went beyond the call of duty.

ACCOUNTABILITY

Bridging the gulf between the acknowledgement of what must be accomplished and actually doing it involves recognition both that one is well equipped to act and has an obligation to do so. Correspondingly, we will discuss the role of expertise and ownership.

Expertise

Both of the GE-ers we interviewed, Bob Wright (the widely admired vice chairman and long-standing CEO of NBC and NBC Universal) and Jay Ireland, emphasized the importance of domain knowledge. In addition, one of our interviewees gave us a firsthand account of Jack Welch, whom this successful businessman regarded as a role model.

We know it has become sport to pick on Jack, but there is no denying he knows his stuff. Jack had been approached about whether he'd be willing to sell one of the GE divisions. Clearly, he already had opinions about all of GE's divisions and said he'd think about selling the one under consideration at a fair price, and he invited the interested party to meet him in New York. The potential buyer arrived at the meeting with a plethora of questions. Welch, unwilling to risk public disclosure of this exploratory conversation, was there alone— with papers strewn before him. The interested party proceeded to ask the most obscure questions imaginable about the division, to which Welch readily responded without referring to his notes. To the person who witnessed this event, it was one of the most extraordinary performances he'd ever seen in business, and a memorable demonstration of expertise.

Organizations don't always fully appreciate the importance of expertise, and the notion of expertise is frequently subject to misunderstanding. One common mistake is to believe that expertise naturally develops as a function of time on the job and acquaintance with varied organizational issues—as if it were that simple. We've seen lots of people who have been on the job for lengthy periods of time who may be proficient in what they do, but are a far cry from expert in their particular domain. They aren't outstandingly skillful in the same vein as Jack Welch. Indeed, after a certain period of time many employees don't seem to get any better at all. This is a problem, both for the individual and for the company.

A second common misconception is to confuse a domain of knowledge, which refers to the content of a discipline, with a field of knowledge, which refers to the body of people who are supplying the data and studying and interpreting the facts.[13] Unduly focusing on the former at the expense of the latter can be problematic. For example, a handful of domain experts can dominate a company's information flow and decision-making networks as self-appointed gatekeepers.

Rob Cross of the University of Virginia McIntire School of Commerce tells of the highly trained microbiologists within a research and development department at a major consumer goods company: This core group of scientists repeatedly rejected risky ideas out of hand, never allowing them to be fully vetted. As a consequence, they dismissed research into low-glycemic foods that slow digestion and prolong a feeling of being full. Ultimately, these foods were developed elsewhere because the experts killed the idea at a very early stage.[14]

Without expertise, without rich, detailed content knowledge that enables individuals to work at the highest levels of proficiency, there is quite a lot that corporations will not be able to do well. And the deficiencies in corporate execution will be especially glaring when the leader is the one who lacks expertise. Leaders who don't really know what "good" means, or who identify "good" with what an expert would regard as mediocre performance, cannot set high work expectations: They don't know what they are. They can't establish standards, they can't adequately judge performance, they can't instruct and develop others, and they can't model what should be done.

Experts have a deeper and more complex understanding of events and circumstances. This provides not only a better template for superior performance, but a richer functional view of the situation, in which they make better use of data to identify and diagnose problems and employ helpful heuristics that reduce the decision space to the most relevant course of action. There also are far fewer fire drills with expert leaders, since they are able to anticipate dangers and intervene more expeditiously than amateurs.

Josh Weston, the quick and incisive former CEO who built ADP into a powerhouse and household name, taught us that great leadership starts with knowing a little math: $39 + 1 > 40 + 0$. Weston's formula is intended for the individual: The $40 + 0$ worker is so busy processing stuff in her 40-hour week that she doesn't stop to think-analyze-improve. The $39 + 1$ person is just as loaded down with work, but by spending 1 hour thinking and planning, he will get more accomplished and generate more improvements in the remaining 39 hours than our unreflective worker will achieve in her 40 hours. But let's take his formula a level higher and apply it to the entire organization.

Imagine forty novice wine tasters trying to improve their sensibilities regarding fine wine. Since none knows more than another, progress will be uncertain and slow. Now imagine that one of the forty is an expert. Not only that, she is a special type of expert: a kind expert like Weston. Kind experts are generous with their time and patient with learners. Weston is known for his excruciatingly long answers to short questions, but he is also known as a wise and considerate teacher. If someone asks him, "What do I do with x?" his reply isn't, "Put it over there." Instead, he asks, "Why? Where did x come from? What will happen when x is in position?"

Since no one learns anything from terse directives, they get much more from Weston, including, "Now that I have explained everything about x, maybe you can find a better way to deal with x so we don't have to move it from *a* to *b*, and thereby rid ourselves of this process." I don't believe there is doubt about which wine-tasting group will become the more discriminating with time if there is a Josh Weston in its midst.

Josh Weston's approach to learning hints at what is necessary for the development of expertise: deliberate practice. You know the old saw about the visitor to New York who asks a man on the street how to get to Carnegie Hall: "Practice, my dear friend, practice." But let's take a quick detour into the rarefied world of chess, a domain in which one of our leaders, Michael Critelli of Pitney Bowes, is quite good. We have some bad news to report to him. World-class chess players are not smarter than less accomplished players.[15] All are intelligent, to be sure, but that doesn't appear to make a difference in the quality of their game. The following quote attributed to the Spanish violin virtuoso and composer Pablo de Sarasate perhaps sums up what does matter:

> A genius! For thirty-seven years I've practiced fourteen hours a day, and now they call me a genius!

Martina Navratilova, in an interview for *Newsweek*, also summarizes what it takes to excel:[16]

> Athletes just do not quit until they get it right, whether it is about shooting free throws or practicing serves or one particular shot. It is getting up when you don't feel like getting up for your training session, it is going to bed early even though you want to go out with friends, it is only drinking a half a beer when you really want to drink two. Everything it takes to get your goal—that's the mentality of an athlete or a successful human being. Period.

Unfortunately, not just any type of practice makes perfect. As we say above, it has to be *deliberate*. In order to improve, individuals need the direct and indirect help of masters who are able to dissect elements of performance and facilitate problem-solving through new trials and feedback. This is what the Juilliard School, for example, is all about. The virtuoso head of prestigious Juilliard, Joseph Polisi, reminds us that, like the mantra in real estate, "Location, location, location," performance excellence requires "Feedback, feedback, feedback"—artistic masters push, making students test themselves, but judiciously intervene before the student breaks. Every organization needs those who are very good at what they do to have a vested interest in others' development, to take the time required to analyze, reflect, and discover with them. This is not unlike the chess player who learns by replaying the moves of masters, trying to figure out reasons for the masters' selections.

Expertise is not a sufficient condition for breakthrough creativity; other factors play a role too. For example, personality variables such as unconventionality, risk-taking, and openness to experience are plausible contributing factors. Cross-training and breadth of experiences across an area also play an important part. For example, creativity expert Dean Simonton found that the musicians who wrote the best operas weren't the ones who wrote the most operas, but the ones who wrote the most music—that is, the most creative people were the most prolific within the discipline of music composition.[17] This is a very good argument for selective exposure of leaders to related areas in order to facilitate novel connections that would be overlooked with more concentrated training—and a good rationale for moving people around the organization some.

Exploring the world a little is a helpful antidote to tunnel vision. Michael Critelli rotates managers around the organization for another reason that we found particularly perceptive and intriguing. He partially does it to refresh leaders' appreciation of the people who work for them by introducing leaders to new employees who have unique sets of abilities. That is, leaders have a tendency to pigeonhole what particular employees are capable of if they remain in one place too long; moving leaders around can reawaken them to human potential.

Ownership

Organizations are microcosms of life, and veterans of institutions will tell you a great deal goes on within them. Leaders recognize the wide range of potential employee behaviors and go to great lengths to ensure that those enacted are constructive. If you think about what makes healthy societies of various types and sizes work well, we think you will conclude that the following clusters of behavior are desirable.

- *Citizenship*: A good citizen promotes the general welfare of the community by voluntarily engaging in behaviors that are discretionary, outside of his particular role or function, and performed without obvious expectation of recompense.

- *Preservation*: A good citizen affirms the physical and ideological foundation of the community by caring for the facilities and equipment and by ensuring that the value system of the community is upheld—by making a "citizen's arrest," if necessary. Indeed, Pete Peterson of Blackstone Group has instituted an honor code that is familiar at some of the premier educational institutions: Those who witness violations of the company's code of conduct (which employees sign annually) but who do not report the incident are subject to dismissal. The idea is that everyone has an active responsibility to protect the organization and what it stands for. And speaking of responsibility . . .

- *Responsibility*: A good citizen feels an obligation to increase the moral standing of the community and to improve the lives of fellow inhabitants by actively contributing to the group's welfare. In essence, a responsible citizen voluntarily does what she can to enhance the functioning of the collective— whatever its purposes.

We want to discuss responsibility further, because it was a hallmark concept in many of our interviews, one that we know is of perennial interest to executives. Everyone knows you need it, but the leaders we spoke to offer some insights into how they achieve it. There is nothing incongruous about the combination of kindness and a willingness to hold people accountable for results.

According to Pete Peterson, the worst thing you can do to undermine accountability is to treat the budget process as a formality, a statistical exercise by which managers apply uniform percentage increases to prior numbers and, *voilà*, believe they have produced a meaningful plan. Rather, the budget process must be an organic one formulated from the bottom up, based on realistic observations and assumptions about markets, products, the economy, and so on. It is this intimate involvement in the process by the entire management team that makes it each person's plan: *his* plan for which *he* is responsible. "People won't feel accountable for outcomes they don't own."

It is a curious fact that something that one can call one's own assumes added value. Richard Thaler, a leading behavioral economist, has referred to this as the *endowment effect*.[18] He neatly demonstrated the effect by showing that people endowed with a good—say, a coffee mug—want over twice the price to sell the good as others are willing to pay to buy it. The value of a good is higher when it is perceived as something that can be lost or given up than as something that can be acquired. This same principle pertains to goals that people work toward in organizations: They assume greater value when people can rightly call them their own.

The operative idea behind psychological ownership is having some control over both what gets accomplished and the way it is accomplished.[19] Active participation in the planning process and subsequent oversight of the necessary resources is one piece of that. But there is much more leaders can do to promote a ubiquitous sense of obligation among the workforce.

- *Forge employee connections to the company*. It is possible to set one's own goals and have resources at one's disposal without feeling particularly compelled to meet those goals. This is partly because it is possible to feel disconnected from the organization (i.e., have no great love) in which one works. Ownership, then, also involves having an affection for the company for which one works.

- *Set a tone*. How many times have you been asked to "Please submit your budgets to Finance by January 15," so the finance department can roll up the numbers and spit out a plan? How many times has a company proposed ambitious objectives in the presence of an ominous behind-the-scenes ambivalence that whispers, "Just wait awhile and this will go away and be replaced by another initiative." Our answer? "Too many times in too many organizations." Therefore, it is important to set a tone that what the company hopes to achieve is important and that there is no chance the leader's aspirations will dissipate soon.

All of our leaders carve out significant portions of time to meet with their managers to carefully pore over projections, assumptions, and needs. Ask any leader what consumes most of her time, and the answer will be, "People."

- *Develop operating rhythms.* One way to cultivate an acceptance of difficult or onerous tasks is to develop habits. Habits can remove some hesitancy and anxiety, and habit is what Bob Wright recommends as a method for encouraging accountability. He institutes regularly scheduled review meetings with the purpose of updating operating conditions and measuring progress, which all top members of his staff must attend. Many companies will report that they do something like this, but we would make two additions to the standard fare: (a) Attendees to meetings don't just show up—there is an agenda to follow, and people need to come prepared with data and other information to buttress meaningful discussion; our experience suggests that this sort of in-depth preparation is not all that prevalent, with the result that many important items remain open for future discussion—nothing ever gets decided! (b) The idea of "rhythm" reinforces a more general way of operating in which certain activities become a way of life versus interruptions or distractions to that life. Therefore, make goal reviews and progress updates a way of life; make performance management a way of life; make customer contact and feedback a way of life. Management processes are made more fluid and natural through the rhythms of habit.

Encouraging ideas and plans from the ranks and giving people the true means to realize them carries a very important message and side benefit. It communicates that good ideas aren't the sole province of technical whizzes in the R&D lab or of executives, and that it is quite possible for suggestions that are consistent with the organization's direction to originate from anywhere in the organization. After speaking with Rick Levin of Yale University, we thought "percolation effects" captures what open-minded, quality organizations are able to do. Once Yale identified internationalism as one of its objectives, ideas on how to operationalize "a global university" began to bubble up throughout the organization. For example, the Admissions Office suggested that foreign students be accepted based on the same financial criteria as domestic students, in order to encourage foreign enrollment. After due deliberation, the university changed admissions policies so that foreign students who met the high academic standards of Yale would receive financial aid as needed, and thereby become able to attend Yale. Foreign enrollment has increased from 2 percent to nearly 10 percent since the policy change. At the same time, the university has found ways to offer its students international experiences as a fundamental part of their education.

Rick Levin is very good at holding strategic conversations. He and the corporation's officers decide on a general direction for the university based on their understanding of facts. They then advocate their position throughout the organization and include other external constituencies, gathering feedback and refining their plans accordingly. When a final direction is unveiled, each stakeholder in the university will know he was heard, ensuring ongoing, constructive dialog and continuing the generation of ideas.

Joseph Polisi describes this general process as "widening the circle." When Juilliard wanted to add jazz to its curriculum several years ago, Polisi first needed the support of the trustees to ensure adequate logistical and financial assistance. Next, he required the input and allegiance of faculty who would be directly affected by programmatic changes, such as the trumpet department. And, finally, he needed the implicit acceptance of the organization following a general announcement of the new program, which was partly obtained by remaining open to suggestions from organizational members and making adjustments as needed as the program unfolded.

Roxanne Quimby, formerly CEO of Burt's Bees, reminds us how to get an organization to move, literally, en masse. When a thriving beehive reaches a certain population size, there is an executive decision that the hive must divide and half of its members move elsewhere. Thus, a new queen and a swarm of followers leave the hive and huddle on a nearby branch awaiting suggestions from scout bees that have been sent out to collect information on alternative sites. Gradually, scout bees who have located desirable new homes recruit uncommitted scouts to their sites, progressively gaining agreement for a particular decision. When a quorum is reached on a new site, the swarm is instructed to start warming their wings for flight. The scouts' famous waggle dance tells them where to go.

To sum up:

- There is a decision to move.

- Information from key members of the group is collected without bias and aggregated.

  - This is an apolitical process involving the open, independent exchange of information.

  - Opinions are formed in the context of established criteria set by the group (nature), i.e., the site has to have certain attributes.

- Ideas are shared with the entire group (enthusiasm for a location is expressed not only through numbers but by the excitement communicated through the bees' dance).

- The entire community is given time to prepare itself for the impending move.

Although Nietzsche believed that madness is the norm in groups, leaders—particularly kind ones—are able to extract the best ideas from each person, optimally combine that information and patiently build consensus, and then convince entire organization to follow. Additionally, stellar companies, such as Ritz-Carlton, are able to use the group process for many purposes: to motivate, fix problems, and underscore corporate values.[20] For example, regular morning meetings to review guest experiences and to address operational issues conclude with "wow stories" that illustrate how someone exemplified Ritz-Carlton's service values. In one instance, a chef in Bali asked his mother in Singapore to fly him in some special eggs and milk for an allergic guest.

CONSEQUENCES

Josh Weston's office contains a number of signed pole vaults, an oddity for a former CEO with no notable history in the sport. You might be surprised to learn that the winning vault in the Olympic Games in Rome in 1960 was by U.S.-born Don Bragg, at 15′ 15″; the winning vault in 2004 in Athens was 19′ 6¼″ by American Tim Mack. No doubt the vaults will go higher. In competitive Olympic sports, an inch a decade is a long way to go.

Pole vaulting is interesting, first, because it is a sport that tolerates failure and, second, because it taunts success. Pole vaulters get three tries to clear a height before being eliminated from the competition, and if they succeed at one height, their "reward" is to try again at a higher height. This sports analogy is especially revealing of two principles central to achieving exemplary results:

- It is okay to fail (but not repeatedly at the same activity).

- You can always do better (but whereas success can be its own reward, it is not the only thing that regulates performance—there are other contingencies as well).

Usually when you try to invent or innovate, failure comes first. Roxanne Quimby duly notes that "Brilliance looks like devastating failure at some point in the process." There is no complete script to follow, no foolproof method. Risking failure is the natural price to pay for progress. Maria Rodale, the creative leader of Rodale Publishing, tells of repeated attempts to reach a new under-forty female magazine readership. After one costly start-up attempt and one acquisition—both of which were shut down—they got it right. Today, that magazine, *Women's Health,* has well over one million subscribers. Robert Price, tracing the history of innovation inside of Control Data, reveals how the legendary Seymour Cray actually failed before successfully producing the supercomputer of the era, the CDC 6600. Lore has it that Cray magically churned out working computers from his skunk works in Chippewa Falls, Wisconsin. As Robert Price tells it, this is very far from the truth. Success required a firm organizational commitment and resolve, as well as an ability to move ahead when one approach didn't work in order to find one that did. And success was achieved by a team, not an individual, although Cray himself is not remembered as the ideal role model of a team player.

Living with failure is acceptable only when leaders are striving to reach an irresistible goal and are endowed with a curiosity for the unknown, and when an unsettled spirit courageously overcomes fear. The fundamental belief is that it is always possible "to go higher," and that premise is firmly embedded in the organizational consciousness. Good leaders reject the status quo and push their organizations to find better ways of achieving their companies' ends. Additionally, when a good company collectively believes that a certain course is both right and necessary, it won't quit until success is achieved. Competitors without the same boldness will founder and fail.

It's easy to imagine the coach of a vaulting team secretly whacking the vaulter with a pole following the first miss. Not very kind, to be sure, and not much of an enticement to set the bar very high, either. Such tactics lead to organizational collusion in which frightened people without imaginations keep their standards at a manageable height in order to avoid condemnation.

The same goal of continuous improvement that allows leaders to try something new also prevents them from becoming trapped into pursuing failing courses of action. If you buy a magazine franchise, say, for a lot of money, the temptation is to make it work no matter what. There are ample business examples of throwing good money after bad, but good leaders use a very simple rule. If the incremental costs bring a company closer to its ideal future state, proceed. If the added expenses won't both produce the results envisioned and simultaneously meet the standards of quality for delivering value to the customer that the company embraces, then stop! John Pepper's lengthy history at P&G qualifies him to say with certainty that this process can be painful, but as long as the process is beneficial to the customer and will yield returns to the company over the long term, the company—P&G in this case—will persist.

Failure Overlooked

There are two types of failure. First, there are the more obvious errors of commission: overt acts that prove false, or don't materialize as expected in other ways (false alarms). For fans of the horror film genre, making a wrong turn is an act of commission that often has bloody consequences. Second, there are acts of omission (misses), perhaps sticking to a course of action to which there are superior alternatives. You are on the wrong road but don't realize it because you have never explored whether there are better routes to follow. It's not that the road you are on is necessarily bad, it's just that there are more favorable avenues.

False alarms are more noticeable than misses and, consequently, taking a bold, affirmative position in organizations is frequently viewed as highly risky. The consequences may be associated with the decisions of specific individuals and are often more readily and immediately apparent, i.e., if you are wrong, you may earn the "stamp of disapproval." Thus, employees aren't naturally inclined to stick their necks out unless a leader makes it clear that intelligent mistakes aren't cause for decapitations. On the other hand, if you don't say anything and the company figuratively goes up in flames, who's to blame? Besides, people who are nearest the fire can escape long before others know the company is being consumed. So, in organizations, doing nothing—even though the prospect of some unforeseen and undetected danger looms—is often perceived (mistakenly) as the safer course.

Good companies, however, invite analysis of this more subtle form of error by omission by constantly questioning and testing assumptions embedded in their operations. For example, one of us conducted a long-term study of who makes the best pharmaceutical salesperson. The operating assumption was that new hires from other pharmaceutical companies or those with health-related backgrounds do. Without revealing the privileged results, that assumption proved false as replicated across time and samples. The company's hiring protocols weren't bad; they just weren't optimal and would never have been questioned had folk wisdom and casual observation been allowed to prevail—and had the vice president of sales not been willing to test the validity of prevailing beliefs.

Disproving existing positions is challenging not only because one must be prepared to be wrong, but also because we humans just aren't very good at it. One of the tenets of science is to seek out falsifying information, but that is precisely what our Homo Sapiens brains don't do particularly well in the real world. Take the following set of symbols: A K 3 7.[21] Next, assume each of these symbols appears on one side of a card, and on the reverse underside of these cards lies one of these same letters or numbers—with a letter paired with a number and a number with a letter. We make the claim that, "If there is an 'A' on one side, then there is a '3' on the other side." What is the minimum number of cards you need to turn over to verify the truth or falsity of that statement, and which ones? Most people say that two cards need to be turned over (which is correct) and that they are the 'A' and the '3' (which is incorrect). In each of these instances, people are looking for *confirming* evidence, data that will support the claim. If you turn over the '7,' however, you will be looking for falsifying, or disconfirming, evidence. And you will need that evidence to ultimately validate, or invalidate, the claim.

Psychologists have noted many other human propensities to search for and evaluate information in a biased manner.[22] In most instances, biases point in directions that the decision-maker already favors or otherwise more personally values, but are based on incomplete information. This can yield decisions that are carelessly scrutinized and adopted over alternatives that are too quickly dispatched.

Companies need a healthy bit of skepticism to combat the impulse to seek out information that supports the current choice. Not much changes by holding steadfastly to the past. Instead, the leaders with whom we spoke prefer to experiment with the status quo in order to highlight the little things they might do differently, rather than waiting to be clubbed over the head by big mistakes of omission.

Doing Better: Process

Continuous improvement requires sound processes. Processes based on the storehouse of organizational knowledge and capabilities force the company to define how it will do its work. That is, routines are expressions of the best, most efficient ways to accomplish organizational objectives. Most importantly, routines impose discipline and define how members of the organization communicate and how operational problems are resolved.

For us, one of the *aha* moments came when we realized the ubiquity of formal processes within our host companies. Further, it made us realize that the specific operating processes used were immaterial to performance improvement, as long as they contained certain elements. Some of the companies train employees using Six Sigma, some use Total Quality Management (TQM), and some, like Smucker's, choose problem-solving procedures developed by specialty consultancies such as Kepner-Tregoe.

Poking at fads that are purported to be the new salvation of business is a journalistic pastime, and rightly so. There have been some doozies over the years such as using the Rorschach (inkblot test) to make selection decisions and organizing T-groups to better acquaint managers with their inner selves.[23] Sometimes, however, criticisms can be misplaced; TQM, for example, always has been an obliging and, perhaps, undeserving target. We don't think the actual program a company adopts matters as much as the way it formalizes communications and problem-solving. In general, the methods involve analyses of interdependencies, testing of causes and effects, making connections to and borrowing from other domains of knowledge, and so forth. The point is that there needs to be a codified way of defining a problem, understanding the implications, and pursuing a resolution.

The obvious advantage of a defined approach to operational and product improvements is building a foundation based on a common language and point of view. As with natural language, common structure and usage permits mutual understanding, engagement, and action. And like natural language, corporate procedures have a prescribed set of rules that define how a discussion is to unfold. Specifically, the process promotes civil discourse under what have been referred to as "swamp conditions."[24] These are conditions in which there are a high degree of ambiguity, multiple actors with conflicting interests, and a range of options.

Specified procedures divert the nature of the conversation away from individual, departmental, or business unit triumph through debate, persuasion, and power toward a process that may be aptly described as joint deliberation.[25] The goal of deliberation is to thoughtfully weigh evidence in an objective manner, and it works best when the ideas of all stakeholders are openly and freely expressed and data, uncontaminated by self-interest, is introduced. This is one of the basic premises of leadership: trying to get the best ideas from the most people and break apart what Bob Wright of NBC refers to as the "concrete middle"—those sections of the company where people are protective of their turf and resistant to change.

Doing Better: Contingency Management

We would be remiss in omitting some discussion of rewards and punishments, which we politely call contingency management, from our discussion of consequences. Put simply, the basic idea is that behavior is initiated and maintained by a host of consequential environmental factors that levy costs and benefits. People do things for which there are both tangible and intangible rewards and avoid engaging in activities for which there are adverse consequences. The general goal is to structure environments so that behaviors that yield better performances are encouraged, and those behaviors that are detrimental—or not very helpful—are discouraged. There are many ways to do this, which have been the topic of many books. We wish to make a few observations.

First, creating contingencies doesn't have to be a harsh process. The preference normally is to increase the frequency of desired behaviors by establishing the requisite positive outcomes rather than simply eliminating unwanted behaviors through punishments. In fact, sole reliance on the latter is a woefully inadequate approach. Telling people what not to do does not automatically elicit the alternative desired behaviors. You'd think it would, but it doesn't. Without reinforcing contingencies, the behaviors the company wishes to promote will not be performed.

There is nothing that prevents a leader from complementing performance critiques with social support, supervision, and other forms of assistance. Josh Weston encouraged division managers whose performance was lagging to seek out advice from managers who confronted similar problems and obstacles and who could recommend what might be done to improve.

Second, whereas fair compensation has its place, leaders are well aware of its limitations. Not one of our interviewees mentioned compensation as a means to regulate behavior and to focus employees' attention on what is most important. Getting paid is important, of course, as is being rewarded for work well done. Leaders know, however, that there is much more to motivation than the mechanical application of monetary contingencies. For one thing, no set of contingencies could possibly account for the myriad, complex behaviors that must be executed each day in organizations. We refer to corporate attempts to account for and reward every singular behavior through money (or its equivalents, such as stock) as the *Three Stooges Effect.* Called upon as plumbers to fix a leaky faucet, Larry, Curly, and Moe successively attach pipes until they have created an extensive web of piping throughout the home, the last of which leaks. All they succeeded in doing was continuously transfer the leak to a different place and upset the homeowner. Behavior is like the water: try to control it and it finds its own outlets. Poor leaders are like the Stooges, who end up fleeing as the shareholders seek the culprits who sought only remedial, short-term fixes.

Good leaders realize that the best results are intrinsically motivated: that is, guided by a person's reason and internalized values. Highly motivated, achievement-oriented people can be self-sustaining for lengthy periods of time, requiring only periodic motivational boosters and occasional pit stops for tune-ups and repairs.

The best leaders are able to keep employees engaged and performing with the throttle open. We agree with Mike Critelli, however, that one of the great myths regarding corporate performance is that "happy employees are productive employees." Management research would corroborate his claim.[26] However, we believe that the reverse is true: that productive employees are happy. And, fortunately, employees in high-performing organizations with exemplary leaders have plenty of opportunity to be productive.

This is true because such organizations are highly selective as to whom they will hire, accepting those who are smart, eager to learn, and interested in achieving great things. The indefatigable Rick Goings of Tupperware looks for people who can change the weather and not just report it. Thus, employees are stimulated by similarly minded and motivated individuals who collectively create a dynamic workplace where the people are curious and engaged. They have a chance to be productive because companies expend tremendous resources on employees' growth and closely monitor their development. Opportunities in the form of formal training (in-house and outsourced), support for participation in professional societies, and special assignments and projects abound. And in good companies, all of these skill-enhancing exercises are integrated and thoughtfully timed and applied for optimal benefit.

Finally, employees have the chance to be productive because they are given progressively greater responsibility, typically through promotions. The promotions are predominantly internal and go to those who are most deserving, based on past performance and preparedness—not on how long someone has been on the bus (tenure) or to which clubs people belong (favoritism). All leaders will admit that their decisions for promotions aren't always correct, but good leaders will have instituted rigorous review procedures and will have tried to remove as much noise from the decision process as possible. We could say that in this particular arena, our kind leaders are ruthlessly meritocratic. By the way, policies of promoting from within make sense only when the company has valid selection methods, strong developmental programs, quality learning systems, and fair performance processes. Otherwise, deeply flawed promotional practices are likely to lead to inbred mediocrity.

Doing Better: The Opposite of Listening

All great leaders are superb listeners. But there is another valuable side to listening that is particularly important in shaping meaningful exchanges and quality performance: talking. The opposite of listening isn't not listening, but rather talking and making sense. Many of the leaders we have met over the years are pleasant, well-intentioned individuals. But when they are sitting across the table with their eyes trained on you, oblivious to all else but your presence, you start to think, "Hey, he is really listening to me. I had better say something intelligent."

Thus, listening itself provides incentive for another to speak clearly and use all of the facts on hand. If you visit with one of our leaders, you'd better go well armed with evidence and sound argument, because they will accept nothing less. "Just the facts, Ma'am," as Sergeant Friday on *Dragnet* would say. We asked leaders what the worst thing a person who missed her numbers could say to them. To a large degree, the question was incomprehensible to them, since what they expect to hear is the truth and not anything else—and they are not so far removed from the facts to be surprised, at any rate. Good leaders—yes, even kind ones—measure results. No matter what you are trying to do—lose weight, jump higher, improve shareholder return, add a point to market share, use less electricity—unless you measure, there is no chance of improving.

For kind leaders who listen, the difference is that they don't use numbers as blunt instruments to castigate and blame. They see measures as organization-wide indices of performance that require collective analyses and problem-solving. The head of a business unit, for example, may be accountable for achieving certain results, but that doesn't imply that he doesn't deserve aid and will be left dangling. Other people, and maybe additional resources, will be put on the case to help resolve the problem. There is no career penalty for getting assistance from those who may have experience and insight into the problem you are trying to fix. If, in your organization, you are reluctant to ask for help for fear of appearing weak or because of possible repercussions, ranging from public belittlement to career suicide, there is something very wrong with the leadership. If you are a leader in that type of organization, don't believe a word you hear.[27]

NOTES

1. Mankins, M.C., & Steele, R. (2005). Turning great strategy into great performance. *Harvard Business Review*, July-August: 65–72.

2. Gibson, J. (2003). Between truth and triviality. *British Journal of Aesthetics*, 43: 224–237.

3. Cited in Raelin, J. (2006). Finding meaning in the organization. *MIT Sloan Management Review*, 47: 64–68.

4. Bogle, J. (2003). Chasing the rabbit. (http://www.vanguard.com/Bogle_site/sp20030614.html).

5. Vallerand, R.J., Salvy, S., Mageau, G.A., Elliot, A.J., Denis, P.L., Grouzet, F.M.E., & Blanchard, C. (2007). On the role of passion in performance. *Journal of Personality*, 75: 505–533.

6. Shusterman, R. (2001). Art as dramatization. *Journal of Aesthetics and Art Criticism*, 59: 363–372.

7. Novitz, D. (2001). Participatory art and appreciative practice. *Journal of Aesthetics and Art Criticism,* 59: 153–165.

8. Rigby, R. (2007). Buildings of beauty to lift the corporate soul. *Financial Times*, December 4: 16.

9. This formulation for behavior change comes from Ajzen, J., & Fishbein, M. (1980). *Understanding Attitudes and Predicting Social Behavior*. Englewood Cliffs, NJ: Prentice Hall.

10. For comprehensive discussions of framing effects, see Chong, D., & Druckman, J.N. (2007). Framing theory. *Annual Review of Political Science*, 10: 103–126; Druckman, J.N. (2001). The implications of framing effects for citizen competence. *Political Behavior*, 23: 225–256; Levin, I.P., Schneider, S.L., & Gaeth, G.J. All frames are not created equal: A typology and critical analysis of framing effects. *Organizational Behavior and Human Decision Processes*, 76: 149–188.

11. Tversky, A., & Kahneman, D. (1981). The framing of decisions and the psychology of choice. *Science*, 211: 453–458.

12. In generating these comments, we benefited from the following works: Latham, G.P., & Locke, E.A. (2006). Enhancing the benefits and overcoming the pitfalls of goal setting. *Organizational Dynamics*,

35: 332–340; Locke, E.A., & Latham, G.P. (2002). Building a practically useful theory of goal setting and task motivation. *American Psychologist*, 57: 705–717.

13. Simonton, D.K. (2003). The scientific creativity as constrained stochastic behavior: The integration of product, person, and process perspectives. *Psychological Bulletin*, 129: 475–499.

14. Cross, R., Hargadon, A., Parise, S., & Thomas, R.J. (2007). Together we innovate. *Wall Street Journal,* September 15–16: R6.

15. Ericsson, K.A. (2005). Recent advances in expertise research: A commentary on the contributions to the special issue. *Applied Cognitive Psychology*, 19: 233–241.

16. Peterson, H., & Kantrowitz, B. (2006). Lessons we have learned. *Newsweek*, September 25: 74.

17. Simonton, D.K. (2000). Creative development as an acquired expertise: Theoretical issues and an empirical test. *Developmental Review*, 20: 283–318.

18. Thaler, R.H. (1980). Toward a positive theory of consumer choice. *Journal of Economic Behavior and Organization*, 1: 39–60.

19. For a comprehensive examination of the psychology of ownership, see Pierce, J.L., Kostova, T., & Dirks, K.T. (2001). Toward a theory of psychological ownership in organizations. *Academy of Management Review*, 26: 298–310; Pierce, J.L., Kostova, T.R., & Dirks, K.T. (2003). The state of psychological ownership: Integrating and extending a century of research. *Review of General Psychology*, 7: 84–107; Pierce, J.L., O'Driscoll, M.P., & Coghlan, A. (2004). Work environment structure and psychological ownership: The mediating effects of control. *Journal of Social Psychology*, 144: 507–534.

20. Gallo, C. (2007). How Ritz-Carlton maintains its mystique. *BusinessWeek Online*, February 14.

21. Wason, P.C., & Johnson-Laird, P.N. (1972). *Psychology of Reasoning: Structure and Content.* Cambridge, MA: Harvard University Press.

22. Bazerman, M.H., & Chugh, D. (2006). Decisions without blinders. *Harvard Business Review*, January: 88–97.

23. Colvin, G. (2004). A concise history of management hooey. *Fortune*, June 28: 166.

24. Rosenhead, J. (1992). Into the swamp: The analysis of social issues. *Journal of the Operational Research Society*, 43: 293–305.

25. Franco, L.A. (2006). Forms of conversation and problem structuring methods: A conceptual development. *Journal of the Operational Research Society*, 57: 813–821.

26. Iaffaldano, M.T., & Muchinsky, P.M. (1985). Job satisfaction and job performance: A meta-analysis. *Psychological Bulletin*, 97: 251–273.

27. In his classic work, Hirschman argued that if employees are not able to voice opinions, and if leaving the company isn't an option, the only alternative is to simply go along with things: Hirschman, A.O. (1970). *Exit, Voice, and Loyalty: Responses to Decline in Firms, Organizations, and States*. Cambridge, MA: Harvard University Press.

THE TRUTH MATTERS

George Washington could not tell a lie. According to Mason Weems, our first president as a boy confessed to cutting down the cherry tree.[1] This parable about truth-telling was designed to impress upon the youth of the time the importance of honesty. And who better to serve as a symbol of honesty than the most revered leader of his times, George Washington.

In an historic about-face, over two hundred years later, presidential figures are desperate to convince us of their honesty. September 2007 marked the month in which the Honest Leadership and Open Government Act became law, thereby codifying an act with the longest string of oxymorons in its title. The pervasive attitude is that often leadership is not honest, and governance is rarely open, whether in the public or the private sphere.

It is refreshing, then, when the unvarnished truth is conveyed by someone who is in a position to conceal the facts. For example, as the subprime mortgage fiasco took hold in 2007, Oakmark's Select Fund chief Bill Nygren watched the value of his portfolio decline. In an especially candid note to shareholders, Nygren called attention to the portfolio's performance, describing recent returns as "dreadful."[2]

In contrast, the implosion of Bear Stearns & Co.'s hedge fund (and, ultimately, Bear Stearns itself) due to the same mortgage crisis that afflicted Nygren's fund has thus far resulted in 17 investor lawsuits. At issue is whether the funds soft-pedaled the real risks of the investments. Plaintiffs will argue that Bear Stearns downplayed the risks and that, on at least one occasion, it likened these highly leveraged funds, partially backed by subprime mortgages, to ordinary bank accounts.[3]

The fact that Nygren's revelations seem quaintly heroic in contrast to the well-understood temptation to fudge the truth about problematic details anecdotally suggests that the vision of honesty personified by George Washington has yet to completely catch on in business. As it happens, people lie all the time—on average one to two times every day.[4] For example, we don't excuse ourselves from a tedious bore at a cocktail party by boldly stating our true reasons; we politely ask his indulgence as we refresh our drink or catch an old friend before she slips away. We lie as a social lubricant, which is superior to the alternative. As opposed to such unremarkable lies and other tall tales we may relate with a wink, dishonesty in business undermines a prerequisite for organizational success with a vengeance.

As we will discuss throughout this chapter, dishonesty comes in all shapes and sizes. The common denominator, however, of all forms of dishonesty is a fundamental failure to recognize the existing facts, regardless of whether you deceive yourself or others.[5] Andy Stern of the Service Employees International Union said it best when he told us that the best way to change perception is to change reality, not create an alternative universe. Thus, parsing words, splitting hairs, or euphemistically disguising the true state of affairs with softball phrases will not produce change. A leader's displeasure with the facts won't change them. Pete Peterson alluded to this misbegotten strategy when he rhetorically asked us, "Reality always wins out, doesn't it?" Andy Stern admonishes, "Speak dramatically, speak clearly, and speak honestly. One of the worst things a leader can do is fake reality."

Dick Parsons of Time, Inc., adds to this consensus viewpoint, claiming that the biggest mistake a leader can make is to be deceptive in any way; ultimately, others see what there is to be seen, and this collective intelligence prevails.

Like an elaborate Ponzi scheme that unravels, the truth always has a way of expressing itself in the end. But this end is often too late. Success in life as well as within the corporation requires a respect for reality from the start. Unfortunately, that respect doesn't always make the truth less painful, but it does enable us to arm ourselves with our best defense: our intelligence. In correcting the errors of our ways, truthfulness does allow us to develop our capacities so we thrive as best we can despite difficult conditions.

It is impossible to advance unless you honor the truth of your situation, your capabilities, and the resources you need to both hone your skills and successfully move forward. Private investor Jesse Fink is an accomplished skier who occasionally leads groups of friends and associates of various talents down the slopes. His method of leading these adventures reflects his management style. He starts out at the front and leads the expedition until each person in the party knows the places to meet en route to their final destination. He then drops to the back, allowing the skiers to find their own way down (e.g., through trees, on established routes, etc.), and makes sure no one veers off course. He calls it "leading from behind," which emphasizes two key values: (1) inspiring and (2) empowering others to give their best effort and produce the best results they can.

As a part of our interview with Fink, we speculated about how messy the descent could be if it were based on false assumptions about the difficulty of conditions and the skills of the skiers. Those who were capable might play it safe, and overconfident others might never make it to the bottom. The precondition for a thrilling ride is to push some and hold others back: to help each assess her or his capabilities, given the circumstances, and then permit that person to pick a route consistent with the realities. Clearly it does a leader no good to misrepresent reality—whether to customers, supplies, or employees. Some companies will stagnate and others will die.

Given the importance of facing the facts in both organizational and personal development, it seems reasonable to ask why misrepresentations, distortions, and other ways of concealing the truth abound. There are many reasons. We will begin by discussing why those in business would want to fool or mislead others; a subsequent section will examine why we deceive ourselves.

DECEIVING OTHERS

A physician has just informed you, in confidence, that a close friend of yours has inoperable cancer. The friend, who recognizes that she is not in the best of health, feels great and has only a remote suspicion of the severity of her diagnosis. The doctor offers no evidence about the status of your friend's health, suggesting to the patient instead that more tests are needed and that she will have to be watched closely over the next several weeks. Do you—or the doctor—allow your friend to live out her days with the assumption of a sunny future, or do you tell her the tragic news, perhaps filling her final weeks with unbearable sorrow? Asked differently, if it were you, would you want to know?

If it were you, we suspect that you would want to know, because no matter how bad the news, you would want to be considered worthy of hearing it, and although there will be no happy ending, there will be words to be said to the people you love and details to attend to. You will be better off and more fondly remembered for having been told the truth.

And yet we find it hard to say, for example, that our company provides awful customer service (preferring, "we're no worse than anyone else"), that an employee has "'weaknesses' that need shoring up" (casting shortfalls as "developmental needs"), or that earnings growth has precipitously fallen (opting for the softer language of "slower growth"—probably "temporarily" at that). Any time we become evasive about the truth, we make the same assumptions about employees that the doctor makes about our ailing and unknowing friend: that the truth is too frightening to confront and that the people of the organization are incapable of doing anything about it.

Guarding the truth prevents companies from realizing their potential—it's one reason, at least. It is not possible to enlist employees' support for a problem they do not know exists. Thus, in a *Harvard Business Review* article, Ginger Graham, former group chairman of Guidant, plainly notes the direct relationship between corporate transparency and solutions.[6] Guidant routinely shared financial data, competitive information, market trends, and quarterly successes and failures, reviewing what happened, and why. Graham tells how employees responded with ideas and offered ways to approach difficulties that the company faced and how they would rally when the company was in a pickle. When a product introduction (a medical device) succeeded far beyond expectations—a good problem to have—it was revealed that production would fall considerably short of demand. Without increasing production, the company would not be able to fill orders—a bad problem to have.

As was Guidant's custom, executives called a companywide meeting, informed employees of the problem, and explained what an adequate supply of the product would mean for doctors and their patients. A significant increase in production was the only conceivable remedy, but the company would pursue this course through volunteerism, not by force. In return, the company would do whatever was within its power to ease the burden for those who worked overtime.

Employees offered plenty of ideas, and the company happily complied; the result was record quarterly earnings due to the much-needed delivery of an important medical technology.

Exactly how open corporations should be with employees is a debatable subject, with proponents of open book management asserting, "Very open."[7] Indeed, there are practitioners of this approach within our sample. Anyone can go online to have a look at Yale University's strategic plan; Smucker's publicizes its strategic and financial information for employees. Even if you don't have the same degree of enthusiasm for such openness, one thing is certain: If you want people to help the company, they have to have sufficient information in order to do what is needed. They have to know what the problems are and understand theories about why the problems exist and the effects the problems are having on the company's operations. And employees must have the latitude to think about and act upon those problems.

Shading reality shows a profound disrespect for both the character of people and the value of facts. Individuals need challenges to overcome, and living slightly off center as opposed to in quiet comfort makes us feel alive. Companies that create environments of faux bliss will get little in return.

I Don't Want to Hear It

The people of the organization sometimes sugarcoat their reports to leaders when leaders have implicitly or explicitly made it known that they don't want to hear that the company is experiencing difficulties. In contrast to our kind leaders, who want the facts as people see them, flawed leaders view bad news as too great a personal affront or too anxiety-provoking to regard as welcome. If to preserve a fragile ego, a leader takes the stance that he can do no wrong, then over time employees will oblige him and offer only glowing reviews, while hiding important but negative information. Such leaders are consequently kept in the dark as onlookers await a misstep and fall.

Once the whitewash begins, a culture of obfuscation soon materializes. The organization gingerly tiptoes through minefields, reporting that all is well even as they hear explosions in the distance: evidence of what happens to people who dare tread too close to reality.

Lead Us Not Into Temptation

Perhaps the most obvious reason people within organizations cheat and lie is because either it is in their short-term interest (usually financial) to do so, or they are covering up unethical behavior. Some organizational strategies—for instance, transferring discretionary income between quarters, timing the sale of assets to offset poor quarterly results, accelerating the production of goods to meet quotas (even when there is no market for them), deferring expenses in order to hit forecasts, etc.—are perfectly legal, although one could reasonably question the intellectual honesty of these maneuvers and whether they are helpful or injurious to the company.

Bob Lane, the CEO of John Deere, reminds us that *how* a company does business is its essence. He tells of a meeting with a large African agency that was interested in purchasing Deere equipment. The agency director assured the company that it would secure the order only if it was willing to demonstrate a little more . . . ahem . . . *flexibility*. If Deere couldn't obtain the order honestly, it didn't want it. Paying bribes is not the way it conducts business.

John Deere and Company lives by the rule, "No smoke, no mirrors, no tricks . . . straight down the middle." That means no cutting corners, no dissembling, no exaggerations: just the real deal. That means being earnest with analysts, investors, customers, employees, and others who have a stake in the company, even if the information that is conveyed will not be well received.

Five years ago, Deere shared its strategy with its broad-based distribution network of dealers to ensure that the dealers would be in a position to continue to serve the increasingly complex needs of their customers and stay current with highly advanced technologies. During the five year period, all dealers were being asked to understand the implications of such a critical transition. Some dealers likely were going to acquire others and grow; some dealers might choose to be acquired. The net result was going to be a more consolidated and more capable dealer channel for the customers and the company.

Any company that has modified its sales channels understands the anguish this can cause, particularly when it involves close, long-standing customers. Deere provided an honest assessment of the circumstances, a clear rationale for change, and a reasonable time frame for those who might be affected to prepare accordingly.

It is impossible to be an effective leader if you are unable to make these types of decisions—and kind leaders make them all the time. But the decisions are executed in a humane way. What are the alternatives? A company persists with its current operating model and hopes the problem goes away. Or it can dither about the decision until executives are left with no choice but a quick and painful hatchet job. A leader may absolve himself of responsibility in the latter case by hauling out the "I had no choice" excuse. However well intentioned the postponement of tough, necessary decisions, the end result to those affected is seldom interpreted as kind. As Josh Weston warns, "You don't help matters by sweeping difficult issues under the rug; you are just delaying what will be a far more painful ending."

In order to offset temptations to take advantage of loopholes in systems or engage in covert unethical behavior—and subsequently lie about it—for the purpose of personal gain, in the form of either reward or avoidance of punishment, we offer the following list.

- *Don't invite transgressions*: Impossible goals combined with tantalizing rewards is a bad mix; such circumstances invite cheating, since there is likely to be no return for playing fairly.

- *Establish a culture of trust*: There is a fine line between judicious oversight and spying. It is important to have good monitoring systems in place so that people act responsibly with the organization's assets and recognize the proper management of those assets as a corporate value. Too loose oversight invites the wasting of assets, or worse. Under too strict oversight, employees will fail to see their stewardship as a privilege entrusted to them.[8]

- *Underscore the* how *in addition to the* what: The fun of business is trying to figure out *how* to best satisfy customers' true needs, knowing that if this is done properly, the *what* will follow. Concentrating solely on the what may not only encourage aberrant behaviors to meet objectives, but result in self-defeating behaviors as well. One way to increase profits is to reduce costs by using, for example, lower-grade ingredients or materials. But sacrificing quality in order to gain short-term increases in profits is not a smart way to retain customers.

- *Model appropriate behaviors*: Ultimately, the measure of anyone is in what she does. For leaders, people are watching, and how you conduct yourself in public will have immeasurable effects on others.

MOSTLY HARMLESS SELF-DECEPTION

When we were growing up, one of the worst things you could call someone was a fool. This was considered much worse than other four-letter words and was reserved for those on a collision course with reality who were too blind or too dumb to see it coming.

We as a species appear to be hard-wired for a degree of self-deception: We lie to ourselves quite naturally. These little lies serve to protect or elevate our esteem, either toward ourselves (self-enhancement) or in the eyes of others (self-presentation). We adeptly manage our self-images so we appear more virtuous and competent than objectively warranted. We do this in three ways.[9]

Self-Serving Attributions

Both positive and negative events occur in our lives, at home and in the workplace, and although the reasons for these events may be uncertain, we nevertheless attempt to explain them by assigning causes. There is an overwhelming bias to these attributions. People tend to attribute positive outcomes to personal factors such as ability or effort, and negative outcomes to external factors such as bad luck or insufficient resources. In essence, people take credit for favorable results and deny responsibility for unfavorable results.

The Better-Than-Average Effect

Places like Garrison Keillor's fictional Lake Wobegon, where everyone is above average, are everywhere. Studies have shown that self-evaluations of traits, abilities, and performances are uniformly higher than if evaluated by others or based on an independent assessment of the facts. That is, although it is logically impossible, most people view themselves as better than average across a wide range of dimensions. This is one reason why people tend to be unreceptive to average to below-average performance feedback—because the information is unbelievable to them. In turn, anticipated resistance is why such feedback is so difficult to give.

The Bias Blind Spot

An attempt to bolster or affirm self-regard would not be effective if we knew we were doing it. That is, the process has to coincide with a capacity to not notice. Typically, though people believe that others are vulnerable to bias and distortions, we think that we are not so affected. Miraculously, we see ourselves as more objective and self-knowing than others.

The research in psychology shows that all of us are susceptible to mishandling the facts, to some degree. Most of this is harmless stuff that makes us feel good about ourselves without endangering ourselves or harming others. But there are times when our deflective shields are clinically subversive, and that's when organizations need to start worrying.

BAD SELF-DECEPTION

There is a wealth of clinical data on how we deceive ourselves. Invariably, self-deception involves disassociation from an act by either removing ourselves from it or minimizing its relevance: We didn't do it or it's not that important, respectively.[10] We summarize these tactics using more familiar lay terms: denial and distortion.

Denial

For guilt-ridden folk, one way to deny is to wipe an act out of your mind. Don't think about what you did, or choose to think about it at a more convenient time—later: much later. In business, though, there are far more ubiquitous and effective means. Pretending not to notice the elephant in the room is one way. We both have been in our fair share of meetings in which everyone preferred to talk about everything but the most trying and central concerns. John Pepper tells us that P&G breaks through these stalemates by saying, "There is a moose on the table." You can imagine a table of executives in the round, bobbing, weaving, and discussing around the slender legs of a moose, craftily dodging the evident facts that stand before them. Alerting the group to the moose on the table is a safe way to redirect attention to the most pressing and difficult issues.

Blaming others is another prominent mechanism of denial, and it comes in a variety of shapes and sizes, from "just taking orders" to "lousy teammates" to "too heavy a workload" to "the moons of Jupiter weren't aligned." Blaming others is interesting, because blame can have a highly irrational quality that others unwittingly accept. Several years ago, O'Malley took his two kids (a girl, 12, and a boy, 7) out in a paddleboat on a park lake just outside of New Orleans. It was a beautiful, sunny summer day. In the middle of the lake was a fountain that shot out volumes of water in an arc. All three peddlers simultaneously had the same idea: Let's go through the falling waters of the fountain. They entered at the apex of the downpour, where the rush of water was greatest, and were pummeled by its force, making it difficult to breathe and hard to escape.

When they at last broke free, the boat had sunk to its rim, so that they were half submerged as they paddled to shore (it seems that paddleboats are buoyant enough to stay partially afloat). The park police and the manager of the boat service were awaiting their arrival.

O'Malley's daughter was old enough to sense the drama and worried how the wet threesome would gracefully exit the situation. It was a fine mess. O'Malley spoke to the kids as they moved closer to the expectant crowd. "For the record, we are total idiots." "But," his daughter pleaded, "what are we going to tell *them?*" "Well," O'Malley replied, "I'm going to blame them for what happened." And as they disembarked and hauled the bloated paddleboat ashore, O'Malley's first words of exasperation were, "Wow! That really is dangerous. You should put some buoys or something around that." It wasn't his finest hour, and he hopes it was a negative lesson with lasting positive value for his children. It is to this day a very memorable experience for them. But it does show how culpability can be shifted to and accepted by other parties. Oh—after ruminating about their possible negligence and regret that they hadn't cordoned off the fountain, the park authorities asked the family to kindly leave the park.

Basically, disengaging yourself from an unethical or disastrous act presumes that you either had nothing to do with it (I wasn't there, I had no part in the decision) or aren't to be held accountable (there was nothing else that could be done, I didn't mean to do it, it was someone else's fault), when, of course, a reasonable person might meaningfully attach you to the event.

Distortion

There are several ways in which we can admit to doing something but minimize the wrong perpetrated or the damage done. One of the less obvious ways is to compartmentalize activities into separate buckets, each with its unique rules. Thus, while all may be fair in love and war, the rules of engagement aren't as permissive in other aspects of our lives. In business, because it is "business," it may be tempting for people to give themselves more latitude for cunning and deceit than they do at home simply because the purposes and behavioral guidelines are perceived as distinct.

In a recent episode of *The Office*, the head of the regional office accidentally hits an employee with his car in the parking lot, fracturing bones and putting her in the hospital. But good news: While she is in the hospital, another life-threatening affliction is discovered and, as the head of the office *rationalizes*, hitting her with his car was good, not bad, fortune. The negative aspect of the wrong is offset by a good that counterbalances it.

There are many other methods we use to cloud transgressions or bonehead decisions. The last one we will mention before moving on to a discussion of the ill effects of self-deception on corporate functioning is faulting the victim, who, in organizations, is frequently the customer. To some extent, this maneuver transfers blame to the "stupid" customer, who doesn't understand your position or what you are trying to accomplish. But this technique also assumes the mistakes or misdeeds are idiosyncratic to particular individuals and that the harm done when spread across customers is not that bad, really: It's isolated to a few malcontents, and a systematic response isn't required.

MORE PROBLEMS WITH DECEPTION

Clearly, no constructive organizational responses can occur when problems or a sense of accountability for their solutions aren't recognized. Given the enormous organizational consequences of sugarcoating facts, the former CEO of Gillette and Nabisco, in a recent keynote address, flatly gave his audience this advice: "Tell the truth."[11]

Misrepresentation of facts might make them temporarily more palatable, but it won't change them. And when the leader is the fool, it is all the more problematic for the company, because such leaders have insidious ways of keeping unpleasantries at bay throughout the company. They allow a ripple effect of falsehoods and excuses based on clear signals from the top that if the emperor has no clothes, no one had better dare mention it. Self-deception creates companies of dupes and yes-men who find it increasingly easy to do the unmentionable and ignore the necessary, because they have become practiced at explaining it all away.

And, thus, to us and to our interviewees, the master of dishonesty has committed one of the most grievous organizational sins. He has asked us to be conspirators in his enterprise in which people function according to a grand fiction. There is nothing in this for us. The portrait of a person who is asked to cut both ethical and operational corners and who is too fragile to meet genuine challenges is not a flattering one. In contrast, when Michael Cherkasky became CEO at Marsh & McLennan, he sent the following message to employees: "We will win in the marketplace and we will do it the right way!" The underlying message is, "We have a great challenge before us, but I am confident in our abilities to succeed, and I know that we are the kind of people who our customers will appreciate doing business with." Leaders convey a great deal to followers, but nothing more important or fundamental than expressions about who they are and what they are capable of.

TRUTH, SELF-AFFIRMATION, AND THE LEADER AS ARTIST

In this section, we'll draw some parallels between leadership and art, and some readers may find that strange. At one level, we use similar-ities as literary devices to make our points. But the primary reason is that we believe leadership and art have the same goal. They both ask us to look at the world in a different way and to engage with it. They both challenge us to think more deeply and fully about the human experience, what we want for ourselves, and what we hope to be.

Maria Rodale calls it "living in the world." In his 2007 commencement address at Stanford University, poet Dana Gioia, the chairman of the National Endowment for the Arts, concluded by saying, "Art awakens, enlarges, refines, and restores our humanity." We would add, "So does leadership." Both are expected to fulfill eudaemonistic functions of enriching our lives. This entails producing new insights, realizing values, and awakening slumbering emotions, not simply seeking delight, so as Rick Goings says, "People don't die with their music inside them."

In fairness, we aren't the first to note the connection between leadership and art, as both leadership and art have been conceived as imaginative enterprises grounded in basic human truths.[12]

There are several versions of a work of art by contemporary artist Bruce Nauman titled *The True Artist Is an Amazing Luminous Fountain*. The one we have in mind displays these words on a transparent, rose-colored Mylar shade that is hung over a window. The viewer is compelled to look through the wording on the shade in order to see the outdoors and, in so doing, to reflect upon the artist as the generative source of one's vision. Nauman invites us to consider the role of the artist in society, but the fact that we must gaze through a window to see what is already there is, on first glance, suggestive of the self-satisfying cleverness of a modern artist.

If we replace the word "artist" with "leader," we have an equally poignant abstraction with which to probe an essential aspect of leadership: truth. The fact that Nauman's piece applies equally well to both leadership and art is probably indicative of their common heritage.

Each was once similarly conceived as human capacities to make and perform.[13] The burst of discovery and invention and the subsequent spread of knowledge in the Renaissance changed that. Elaborate taxonomies were produced throughout the 16th and 17th centuries that substantially became the topically arranged courses that are used by colleges and universities today. Although it occurred gradually, eventually the arts were carved into two. One category included such pursuits as painting, poetry, sculpture, and music and was variously referred to as the beautiful, the noble, the elegant, the higher, and the polite arts. The term *fine* was ultimately settled upon. The second cluster, which included such activities as masonry, embroidery, woodworking, ceramics, and glassblowing, initially was referred to as vulgar or servile arts—until the more agreeable terms *mechanical* and *practical* were applied and stuck.

On the one hand, there arose an elite class of artists newly freed from their patrons by the growing prosperity among the general populace. Artists now could create whatever they pleased and distribute their works directly to the public through the burgeoning gallery system, symphony halls, publishers, and so on. They no longer had to produce for specific occasions, for specific places, and according to specific criteria.

On the other hand, craftspersons in the mechanical arts worked from precise foreknowledge of an end result, transforming raw materials into products for commercial purposes, using labor as the means. Their world was perceived to be physical, calculative, rule-governed, and unimaginative. Ostensibly they produced, according to design and the materials of their trade, items of a distinctive utilitarian character in exchange for, yuck, money. Most workshops eventually deployed the methods of Josiah Wedgwood. Artists designed the crystal and porcelain; artisans carried out the plans. The schism between "great thinkers"—the artists—and "mere executioners"—the artisans—was complete. Many in the mechanical arts eventually saw their status slip further when machines were able to produce shoes, clocks, bowls, furniture, and an assortment of other utilitarian goods more efficiently and less expensively than people. Many artisans became glorified machine operators.

There arose an artistic caste system demarcated by the amount of independence one had to create images and objects of one's choosing; by the nature and preparedness of the raw materials with which one worked (e.g., artists begin with a blank canvas and often create their own pigments, etc.; artisans are given sheets of metal, leather, glass, wood, etc., to ply); by the degree of labor involved; and by the immediate utility of the outputs.[14] Attitudes regarding the framers and shapers of ideas, to whom the word *genius* was often applied—and adeptly nurtured by the beneficiaries of the moniker—and those whose purposes were simply to produce by prescription were widespread. The former had the latitude for creative expression, and the latter did not. The former were true artists, and the latter were not.

These traditional distinctions drawn between artists and artisans parallel those that have been made between leaders and managers.[15] Leaders predominantly work in the realm of ideas, shaping an organization's direction and impetus, contemplating how best to transform various forms of capital to fit their grand design. These types of leaders have been variously described as idols, heroes, saviors, magicians, and demigods.[16] Managers and employees take materials and use the instruments of their trade to mold and manipulate them according to preexisting procedures, plans, and standards. Many in business still believe that there are certain people who are specially endowed with the gift of clairvoyance and marginalize the creative inputs of the rank and file. A small subset of the organization, largely based on educational pedigree, is chosen for certain select experiences and accelerated development as future leaders. The rest, the putative unimaginative "machinists," must fend for themselves.

With that introduction, we will now discuss eight leadership principles, occasionally using Nauman's piece and other art as metaphorical points of departure.

Principle 1: Craft Matters

Everyone knows the truism that technically skilled people don't necessarily make the best managers. That tidbit, however, obscures the fact that no one wants to be led by someone who is not proficient in her area and who has a scarcity of domain knowledge. That is, we lose sight of the fact that even geniuses have mastered their respective craft. Thankfully, Richard Sennett has resurrected the demonized notion of craft, clarifying that every achievement is predicated on discipline, tenacity, and know-how: in a word, craftsmanship.[17]

Principle 2: Leadership Is Based on the Ordinary

Nauman's work exposes the hubris of the elite class. The use of a fountain as a metaphor for creative genius is a part of the satire. In casting artists as luminous fountains, Nauman is relying on our conventional notions of artists (or leaders) as separate from, or elevated above, the everyday, spewing great truths that are ostensibly unavailable to the rest of us.

Fountains have had a revered place in the arts, ranging from the glorious fountains of ancient Rome to modern-era Paris. The most famous and often discussed fountain in 20th-century art is Duchamp's "Fountain," which is a urinal. Nauman could have compared true artists (leaders) to luminous stars or gemstones, but he chose a fountain instead—and there must be a reason.

Duchamp's urinal is functionally useless, signed by a cartoon character ("R. Mutt"), and dated 1917. One interpretation is that it attacks the arrogance, conceits, and false pride of national leaders, embodied by grand fountains such as those at Versailles. Infatuated by their own greatness and convinced of their own infallibility, the leaders of Europe brought the world to an avoidable Great War, costing millions of lives. Leaders who believe that they are endowed with special insights and powers are dangerous. Proud and self-assured, they reduce states of affairs to simple black-and-white caricatures, to protect false images and to justify conflict and sacrifice. Others are for or against, in or out, and there simply is no middle ground for dialog and compromise.

Principle 3: Leaders Work Invisibly

Fountains are also places where people gather. They serve as focal points for the community—places to sit, to talk, to conduct business, and to play. Fountains are steadfast and reliable fixtures that provide common ground for discourse and exchanges. And while the fountain may be a lure, the action is all around it. Leaders, like fountains, provide a focus for action. They initiate it, encourage it, and structure it, but do not get in the way of it. They spontaneously stimulate the liveliness of a city plaza without themselves becoming the center of attention. They promote the significant life of the community.

What's more, fountains are places for renewal, where we reconnect to our surroundings and to each other. We return to them time and again and feel refreshed. There is a wellspring of hope in the waters of a fountain. We toss in coins to signify as much. Settings for energizing activity, fountains are a source of optimism and strength, nudging us on and ensuring that our forward motion will pay off. (What more could we ask of a leader?)

Environmental psychologists refer to such centers as restorative places, places to which people feel especially attached because they allow them to experience beauty, freedom of expression, and control, without being overwhelmed by external incursions and pressures.[18] Visitors are able to keep their minds clear and focused. We don't see why these places have to be island retreats.

Principle 4: Leadership Requires Introspection

Nauman's work also reminds us that art and leadership act as mirrors. When lighting conditions are right, windows become reflective surfaces, allowing us to catch glimpses of ourselves. This introspective aspect of the arts challenges the viewer to form an opinion, to question why he or she feels a particular way, to come to terms, and perhaps to take a stand. One of the most basic questions a leader can ask himself is, "Why am I reacting this way [to a statement, idea, event . . .]?" It is a question that puts him in control of the situation versus being controlled by it. It may seem "soft," but being in touch means being able to make effective responses.

Great art and leadership challenge: They do not allow us to live easily in states of indifference or neutrality. They knock us off equilibrium, if only momentarily, allowing us to feel more intensely and to live more fully. The genius of Maya Lin's Vietnam Veterans Memorial is that the selected material, black granite, pushes the reflective capacity of art to the limits. Visitors are compelled to see their living images superimposed on the names of the dead. As one examines these dark walls, one cannot help but feel a profound sense of loss for those who sacrificed their lives; this emotion is amplified by the modest descent below ground level viewers must make.

As wrenching as this memorial is, it has become one of the most frequented sites in Washington. Visitors know that they will be moved precisely because they want to remember. Great leadership shares this seductive quality. The messages imparted tend to be enduring. As philosopher Peter Kivy has said, the best messages are those that have lengthy, reflective afterlives: They stick with you and keep you mulling over their significance long after the communication has ended.[19]

Leaders invite us to willingly enter a relationship that sharpens awareness of who we are and what we believe regardless of the nature and depth of those experiences. If leadership and art said nothing to us about us, people would not care much about either. It is because our encounter at the Vietnam Veterans Memorial is highly personal that we seek it out.

Principle 5: Leadership Is Life-Affirming

There is a scene in *Saving Private Ryan* (DreamWorks, Paramount Pictures, & Amblin Entertainment, 1998) in which a unit led by Tom Hanks overcomes a German position, suffering losses in the process. The men in the unit debate killing the one German survivor. Tom Hanks has a decision to make. He can order his men not to shoot or he can look the other way. The first option removes choice and accountability from the men's actions; that is, they never get to decide on what is right and what is wrong—this option might elicit grumbles that it is a crazy war when you don't even get to shoot the enemy. They don't decide for themselves, and so they are free to question and ridicule.

The second option is an abdication of authority in which he essentially transfers his responsibilities to others—an action that will undermine future attempts to maintain order within the unit. Hanks' character knows this is a tough spot to be in, and he understands what the impulses are. But he also understands that in this most horrific of circumstances, this war, there is a life beyond the immediate that he wishes to protect. When this day is over, when the war has ended, he wishes to be whole. So, he chooses a third path when facing his men—he implicitly asks them how they want to think of themselves. They let the unarmed German go.

The best leaders ask us to adopt a new perspective on matters—to see things in new ways—and, further, get others to see themselves as members of communities. The brilliance of the Vietnam Veterans Memorial is that you not only see yourself reflected in the granite facing, but see the line of people standing beside you and the flowers that have been dropped at the base of the memorial. Companies are fond of such sayings as "Everyone must sing from the same sheet of music." That is, leaders expect that they will foster a social harmony in which everyone understands and abides by the rules and aims of the enterprise. Substantive corporate activities such as goal setting are based precisely on this premise. Often, what those leaders instill is conformity and rigidity. People can sing in unison irrespective of any fellow feeling. But such a concept of collectivity is a far cry from the one initiated by the arts or by true leaders. Coordination is not community. The real power of the Vietnam Veterans Memorial is that it makes it possible to mourn with others. Great leadership pulls you toward it and brings people together.

Invariably, great leadership, as with art, is life-affirming. Neither great leaders nor great artists require us to agree with their theses, but they do ask us to contemplate the human condition and to discover in our encounters that which has meaning. You may have your own favorite political speeches, but there is one that stands out for us. It nicely illustrates what we call the self-affirming aspects of leadership.

The speech was delivered by Ronald Reagan following the *Challenger* disaster in 1986. That event was one of the most painful in recent American history, and most people can recall where they were and who they were with when they heard the tragic news that the *Challenger* had exploded. Most people also remember the video footage showing the faces of family and friends of the *Challenger* crew and could feel their immeasurable sorrow. President Reagan encouraged the nation to keep moving forward.

> And I want to say something to the school children of America who were watching the live coverage of the shuttle's take-off. I know it is hard to understand, but sometimes painful things like this happen. It's all part of the process of exploration and discovery. The future doesn't belong to the faint-hearted; it belongs to the brave. The *Challenger* crew was pulling us into the future, and we'll continue to follow them. (Ronald Reagan, January 28, 1986)

President Reagan reminded us that our country was founded on enterprise, adventure, and daring and that despite the inevitable dangers of venturing forth into the unknown, and the temptations to stop, we would not. He didn't obfuscate or fabricate reality. He didn't assuage our insecurities with platitudes or false assurances. In this defining moment, he looked through the window and offered his interpretation of the facts. He asked us to see what he saw. The power of President Reagan's message lay precisely in its connection with the familiar. If there was any appeal whatsoever to the Eternal, it was to those everlasting values that define humanity: to persevere under strife, to reach out with compassion to those in need, to take risks knowing that one may fail.

In a speech before the joint session of the U.S. Congress on December 20, 1941, Winston Churchill, who never minced words, directly asked (with reference to the Germans and Japanese), "What kind of people do they think we are?" And he proceeded to tell us how we should think of ourselves: as people who will persevere against foes that seek our ruin; as people who will defend what is dear to free men and women everywhere; and as people who, although separated by an ocean, will build an unshakable bond to ensure the future safety of the world against the unprovoked pestilences of war.

Principle 6: Leadership Is a Distillation of Chaos

The Nauman piece reminds us that producing stirring images that capture attention requires extraordinary skill. Artists who aspire to be great can achieve that status only through years of study, sustained practice that includes many failures and unfinished works, mastery over their materials, and the capacity to artfully represent limitless possibilities. The frame on the Nauman work that surrounds the window suggests that not everything that can potentially be apprehended is relevant. The scope of observation is invented. The leader, through a series of choices, decides what should be presented and, equally important, what should be omitted. That is, the leader produces a finite message from the infinite. After all, we are bombarded by a myriad of communications each day and must sift through the clutter to find our way.

Thus, it is the leader's job to assemble and depict fragments of reality in a manner that conveys an identifiable message, while simultaneously reducing distractions, i.e., blotting out where people need not look. Keeping the extraneous out of sight and the pertinent in is a fundamental task of the leader. He or she arranges and blends symbols, structures, and communications into a unified whole, imposing order and meaning on daily observation and experience. A messy array of stimuli is distilled to a few ideas, and the leader's work succeeds or fails by the clarity, elegance, and force with which these ideas are related.

Principle 7: Leadership Requires a Novel Way of Seeing

The frame and the colored Mylar covering also signal a purposeful attempt to hold something out as art. Viewers are being asked to suspend their customary way of perceiving and to adopt a particular attitude toward what the leader-artist is trying to accomplish through words, actions, symbols, and such. That is, a leader or artist not only wants others to attend to and observe his representations, but to look at them differently.

The tinted covering over the window indicates that the artist is not simply replicating reality but showcasing it in a certain way so that people will notice. Why else depict houses, hills, roadways, and ponds when there are perfectly good ones in natural settings to look at? Oscar Wilde had a point when he maintained that life imitates art.[20] It is through art that we become more attuned to life, more aware of both our material and our psychological worlds, which are brought into sharper focus.

Here's a thought experiment. Imagine you are sitting on the back patio at work; the patio is composed of cement squares painted different colors. Lots of feet pass over these blocks daily without any notice. But suppose someone comes up to you and says, "That's a work of art!" with reference to the patio. Suddenly, you are asked to look at the patio differently—perhaps to see coloration patterns you hadn't noticed before, well-placed cracks and fissures.

Chances are, in this case, you will ultimately resume your usual relationship with the patio and walk on it, eat on it, and so on. In the end, it may say nothing to you and, indeed, be very bad art, but the presumption that there was something there created a whole new way of perceiving, even if in the end it brought disappointment.

To say that so-and-so is a leader is, similarly, to make a bold statement that solicits a different response. You are hypothesizing that something profound is "there," and, if correct, we should experience emotion of greater magnitude—positive or negative—than we otherwise might. It is at least an invitation, however tentative, to regard the person at issue differently.[21]

There is a painting by René Magritte entitled *The Human Condition*, a painting of a landscape painting that sits on an easel in front of a window. The landscape is arranged to perfectly coordinate with the out-of-doors: The scene through the window picks up where the landscape leaves off, creating the impression of continuity between the two. The onlooker infers that what must be behind the landscape is precisely what the landscape painting depicts.

Magritte's piece forces observers to think more keenly about, and to appreciate more fully, what lies beyond the landscape in ways that simply looking through the window would not. He reminds us that seeing is an act involving imagination, curiosity, and intent. The artist's and leader's mission is to engage our natural human faculties—and this proves remarkably difficult to achieve.

Suppose the landscape on the easel was repositioned to allow a full view of what lies beyond through the window. The work instantly becomes a curio, like a Russian nesting doll: It's a painting within a painting within a painting. In addition, the trail inevitably leads back to the creator—"Look what this clever artist has done!" The work, then, becomes self-congratulatory.

In contrast, great artists are those with the rare ability to invite people into an extraordinarily personal world while remaining anonymous in their work—without getting in the way or disturbing the view. Interestingly, there is very little difference between the original *Human Condition* and the revised painting described above; their relative worth turns on the artist-viewer relationship. In the former, the artist credits the intellect and sensibilities of participant-onlookers and shares something—that's not about him. In the latter, he is reveling in his own virtuosity—the audience is secondarily important. It is all a matter of who is supposed to appreciate whom, but that makes all the difference in the world.

Principle 8. Leadership Is About
Keeping Passion Alive

The word *transformational,* in both art and leadership, generally refers to a work's ability to challenge convention, to open new awareness, inspire new goals, and stimulate actions consistent with those insights and revelations.[22] But there is a more fundamental sense of the word: the ability to help others remain interested in and receptive to what leadership or art has to offer. A large part of what people see depends on what *they* bring to the encounter. Clearly, leaders have the undeniable task of getting results, whatever form they may take. Leaders are hired and paid for precisely that. Nevertheless, if a leader achieves his aims but kills the capacities of others to feel and appreciate, it cannot be good leadership. Good dictators get results.

Too often, when we look through leadership's window, we are introduced to nothing more than necessities and givens through the filter of leaders' feeble vision. Some leaders offer temporary distractions from the pedestrian through their personas. There are versions of the Nauman work in which the saying is scripted in neon, an attention-grabbing material representative of self-promotion if ever there was one: a "good eats" leadership style with flashy facade and plain interior. Indeed, there is no shortage of false leaders who look and act the part but have nothing substantive to offer. Their distinguishing features are their high profiles, the trappings of privilege and status, and self-importance.

Other leaders pander to their audience's proclivities and vulnerabilities through seductive claims and promises, nuggets of praise and money, and the pursuit of transcendent causes without themselves ever feeling connected or a part of a relationship. These leaders attempt to gain favor and get what they want by delivering diversionary pleasures and ethereal satisfactions in place of a genuine life.

When we think of "leaders" we have met over the years, it is hard to say who was disliked more: those who were exceptionally coercive or those who dismissively minimized or refused to acknowledge the work to be done and the conditions in which it was performed. Both are backhanded ways of saying that what followers think and feel does not matter much.

USEFUL LEADERSHIP

Good leadership meets us where we are. True leaders enable us to recognize in their messages those things we care most profoundly about, without distorting or minimizing the essential facts. When observers peer through the Mylar with the boastful inscription on it, they do not see a possible world outside—they see this one. Anyone who has ever done manual labor understands that there is nothing supernatural about a grinder and a press.

The beauty of much art is that it is a part of the fabric of living. Stained glass panels in churches, ceremonial masks, wedding marches, poems that commemorate—all use their special forms to intensify our everyday experiences. Great leadership, like great art, is filled with humanity. And like art, leadership is a human creation that is not so easily divorced from the human condition.

We have met too many leaders who place little value on mixing it up in the "squalid human stew" (to borrow a phrase from Tom Wolfe), preferring to command from afar—often, quite literally, from lofty heights. Given a choice between Heaven and Earth, it appears that Heaven is the more enticing and rewarding option. Like Renaissance attitudes toward craftspeople, we have come to regard those who do useful work as inferior to those who have removed themselves from their company. The result is the curious belief that leadership is somehow unconnected to ordinary activities. This at once bolsters the spiritual significance of one's work and provides the easy excuse that anyone who doesn't understand what leaders have to say and are trying to do is an illiterate slob.

To look through the window in an interested way is to affirm a willingness to be engaged and to participate, to satisfy a desire to learn, to be connected and to feel whole. The people who want in go to the fountain. The person who can draw them there is a true leader. The life of the community depends upon innumerable acts of expression and creation. Most of what occurs in organizations would not be considered "great." Most art and leadership isn't either.

The foundation for organizational excellence lies in many tiny works made possible by leaders who, while pursuing their goals, manage to keep basic human interests and passions alive and intact. Effective leaders intuitively understand that the aesthetic aptitudes that attract others to their message are the very same that enable them to produce creations of their own. Art begets art and leadership begets leadership. As Professor Joseph Rost astutely notes, the best followers are not passive recipients of information who blindly follow instruction. They are active participants in a relationship who have, or will acquire, the very same attributes of the best leaders.[23]

There is nothing illusory about art or leadership. The best of both illuminates our lives, and the resulting effects are as real as being hit by a wave. The true leader is an amazing, luminous fountain, because he shows us something new that always has been right before our eyes.

NOTES

1. Weems, M.L. (1858). *The Life of George Washington; With Curious Anecdotes, Equally Honorable to Himself and Exemplary to His Young Countrymen*. Philadelphia: J.B. Lippincott & Co.

2. Young, L. (2007). Straight talk about bad results. *BusinessWeek*, September 17: 88.

3. Goldstein, M. (2007). Did Bear Stearns soft-pedal risks? *Business-Week*, September 4: 38.

4. DePaulo, B.M., Lindsay, J.J., Malone, B.E., Mohlenbruck, L., Charlton, K., & Coopoer, H. (2003). Cues to deception. *Psychological Bulletin*, 129: 74–118.

5. Smith, T. (2003). The metaphysical case for honesty. *Journal of Value Inquiry*, 37: 517–531.

6. Graham, G.L. (2002). If you want honesty, break some rules. *Harvard Business Review*, April: 42–47.

7. Case, J. (1995). *Open-Book Management: The Coming Business Revolution*. New York: HarperCollins.

8. One of the core ideas behind cognitive dissonance is that actions voluntarily taken become increasingly attractive or acceptable, else why take them in the first place? See Brehm, J.W., & Cohen, A.R. (1962). *Explorations in Cognitive Dissonance*. New York: John Wiley & Sons.

9. Leary, M.R. (2007). Motivational and emotional aspects of the self. *Annual Review of Psychology*, 58: 317–344.

10. Sigmon, S., & Snyder, C.R. (1993). Looking at oneself in a rose-colored mirror: The role of excuses in the negotiation of personal reality. In M. Lewis and C. Saarni (eds.): *Deception in Everyday Life*. New York: The Guilford Press.

11. Whitehouse, K. (2008). "Why CEOs need to be honest with the boards," *Wall Street Journal*, January 14, 2008, R-1.

12. On the connection between the arts and leadership, see Adler, N.J. (2006). The arts & leadership: Now that we can do anything, what will we do? *Academy of Management Learning & Education*, 5: 486–499; Tung, R.L. (2006). Of arts, leadership, management ed-

ucation, and management research: A commentary on Nancy Adler's "The arts & leadership: Now that we can do anything, what will we do?" *Academy of Management Learning & Education*, 5: 505–511.

13. We greatly benefited from the work of Shiner for the ensuing historical overview. See Shiner, L. (2001). *The Invention of Art: A Cultural History*. Chicago: The University of Chicago Press.

14. For an excellent description of craftworks in relation to art, and the obvious parallels to the way we often think of managers and leaders, respectively, see Boden, M.A. (2000). Crafts, perception, and the possibilities of the body. *British Journal of Aesthetics*, 40: 289–301.

15. Zaleznik, A. (1977). Managers and leaders: Are they different? *Harvard Business Review*, May-June: 67–78.

16. This collection of likenesses can be found in Morris, J.A., Brotheridge, C.M., & Urbanski, J.C. (2005). Bringing humility to leadership: Antecedents and consequences of leader humility. *Human Relations*, 58: 1323–1350.

17. Sennett, R. (2008). *The Craftsman*. New Haven, CT: Yale University Press.

18. Strümpfer, D.J.W. (2003). Resilience and burnout: A stitch that could save nine. *South African Journal of Psychology*, 33: 69–79.

19. Kivy, P. (1997). The laboratory of fictional truth. In *Philosophies of Art: An Essay in Differences*. New York: Cambridge University Press.

20. Wilde, O. (1992). The decay of lying: An observation. In P. Alperson (ed.) *The Philosophy of the Visual Arts*. New York: Oxford University Press.

21. The general point made in reference to art can be applied equally to leadership. You can call anyone a leader, but, in doing so, you are asking a lot of the people who are supposed to accept the claim. See Novitz, D. (1996). Disputes about art. *Journal of Aesthetics and Art Criticism*, 54: 153–163.

22. For discussions of transformational leadership, the best place to go to is the authors most closely associated with the theory: Bass, B.M., & Avolio, B.J. (1990). The implications of transactional and

transformational leadership for individual, team, and organizational development. In R.W. Workman & W.A. Passmore (eds.): *Research in Organizational Change and Development*. Greenwich, CT: JAI Press; Burns, J.M. (1978). *Leadership*. New York: Harper & Row.

23. Rost, J. (1991). *Leadership for the Twenty-First Century*. Westport, CT: Greenwich Publishing Group.

GROWTH MATTERS

One common definition of intelligence is an ability to succeed in one's environment. There is quite a lot packed into this definition. To succeed, companies must form symbiotic relations with their environments and detect changes and formulate responses that are essential for their survival. Like species, companies go extinct. The average life expectancy of a large, multinational company is between forty and fifty years; for example, a third of the 1970s Fortune 500 companies were gone by 1983![1] The reasons are manifold, but, typically, economic contractions are attributable to a confluence of factors to which the company did not make an adequate response.

Sometimes companies and their financial sponsors are born dumb and the premises of their businesses are so far-fetched that there never was a chance of market success. And sometimes, technological change is as cataclysmic as a meteor pounding the Earth; the company has too little time to adjust.

But there is a vast region in between in which companies have been blessed with baseline capabilities, a decent product, and sufficient capital and time, yet look on as it all falls apart. For companies to survive and flourish, they must acquire new organizational knowledge and repertoires that enable them to mobilize and react to potential environmental hazards in appropriate ways. That is, they must learn and grow.

ADAPTIVE OPTIONS

Generally speaking, companies have only four ways to adapt at their disposal.[2] This may seem like an oversimplification given the many tomes on strategy, but excluding the strategy of doing nothing, that's really it. Now, of course, execution lies in the details, and we will shortly examine what leaders can do to promote operational excellence, but allow us to first outline the big-picture actions companies can take. Each maneuver is intended to align an organization's goals and capabilities with the demands of the environment.

The most familiar strategy is one of *accommodation*. The company changes itself to meet new environmental threats or to take advantage of new opportunities. Thus, it introduces an innovative product in response to consumer demand, it alters the way it distributes its goods, or it acquires a company to take over a critical piece of the production process where there has been a surfeit of quality defects. When a company accommodates, it adds to or modifies the capacities or attributes of its operations to conform to what is perceived to be the needs of the end users.

A company also can use *assimilation* strategies. A company that assimilates incorporates customer needs into existing operations. Thus, a pharmaceutical company may market a drug designed for one condition as a remedy for another. An auto company may use one tooled platform to produce a vehicular cousin. A fashion company may produce variant generics or private-label goods. A bank may encourage consumers to use its ATM network with the lure of free transactions.

The idea of assimilation is to meet needs by repurposing current capabilities or modifying consumer behaviors to use organizational capabilities for both the customer's and company's benefit. Assimilation is a conservative mechanism in that it assumes that the company's current way of seeing and doing is useful—that its current construction of reality is correct—and that wholesale changes are not required. In contrast, accommodation implies that something profound in the environment and market has changed and that the company's current approaches are no longer viable—its market outlook, product line, and operations must be changed if the company is to survive.[3]

The strategy of assimilation is in many regards similar to the concept of *bricolage*.[4] Using entrepreneurial resourcefulness, the company makes do with novel combinations and applications of what is already at hand or can be scavenged. The difficulty with bricolage is that an individual or organization has to be really smart to employ it well. Think of the old television show *MacGyver*, where actor Richard Dean Anderson, with a few scraps at his disposal, would mount a daring escape, blow up a building, or vanquish a dozen bad guys. Or consider an example from Levi-Strauss that demonstrates the deep institutional knowledge often required for survival. The Coahuila Indians of the desert region of southern California once managed to subsist without ever exhausting their natural resources—without their know-how, the region is truly nearly uninhabitable. Thus, although assimilation may be conservative in the sense that it doesn't entail paradigm-shifting realizations, it does involve smarts, a deep knowledge of available resources and their properties, and a sizable degree of inventiveness.

A third adaptive strategy is *enrichment*. In this case, a company attempts to keep suitors for its customers away; bluntly, the goal is to occupy a monopoly position. One approach is through patent or copyright protections, exclusive licensing agreements, and such. The goal is to create environments suitable only for your organization and to make it as hard as possible for new entrants to emerge in the same space. Pitney Bowes, for example, has patented technologies for its postal apparatus and maintains extremely close ties to postal services around the world, making it very difficult for newcomers to enter its market and succeed. Naturally, size itself can deter competitors: An overwhelming market share can tame others' ambitions. Competitors must either be content with a niche or stay out entirely.

Finally, there always is the option to *exit*. A company can decide that it can't compete in its environment and that no other strategy can cost-effectively rectify that. Thus, under Jack Welch, GE had a rule that if the company couldn't be number one or two in its market, it would get out. There is another slower, more arduous means of exit, and that is gradually becoming a different company with an altogether different market. Thus, today Control Data, for example, is Ceridian: It's still a B-to-B company, but it morphed from a predominantly product-based company to one that is service-based. The idea is that in order to compete, you either become something else entirely or get out at a fair price while you still can.

PREREQUISITES FOR CHANGE

Although companies in the midst of technological and market upheavals may truly believe that the only constant is change—a familiar refrain these days to invoke rapid organizational transformation—in practice all of the adaptive methods are used in combination, and a modicum of institutional stability is a prerequisite for change. While the world outside may seem chaotic, the world inside the organization can't be.

Consider this: For an infant to learn how to reach, she first must be able to control her flailing arms long enough to maintain a goal state, then extend her arm, and finally grab onto an object.[5] That requires coordination of multiple systems (neurological, muscular, cognitive, perceptual), and the simple act really is quite a remarkable systemic process that can easily be thrown off course by environmental interference. The nascent abilities of children provide good analogies for a couple of organizational facts.

First, if a system is totally reactive to environmental conditions and pressures, it will never learn. Like the child, organizations must be able to stabilize actions, if only for a brief moment, if they are to effectively meet goals. Stuart Kauffman, in probing biological order, offers another useful analogy based on a string of Christmas lights.[6] Imagine a large collection of lights—as many as you want, thousands. Each bulb has only one of two states, on or off, and is linked to x other bulbs: Each bulb is to behave the way the majority of its mates behave. Thus, when a given light is connected to three other bulbs, if two or three of these lights are "on," the bulb will turn itself on as well. Otherwise, it will be off. When the lights are instructed to begin randomly flashing, two distinct patterns emerge. When the number of connections is small, the network of lights freezes, and islands of lights remain in the "on" or "off" position. When the number of connections is large, the lights flash chaotically. But here's the thing: When the network is disturbed by flipping a bulb, everything in the chaotic system changes. Completely new patterns appear.

On the other hand, when frozen systems are disturbed, very little happens—the network retains its isolated subsystems and simple repetitive patterns. Systems in constant flux can never retain and transmit any information and, thus, can never stabilize. At the other extreme, ultra-stable systems don't transmit information effectively either, and they, too, never change, or change only marginally. As such, neither system is capable of adaptation. For an organization to be able to change, a condition between chaos and fixation must be achieved.

Second, a system can only do what it is capable of doing. If, returning to the analogy of the child, the neurological system can't align movement with perception, if the muscular system is poorly developed, or if appropriate brain functioning has not yet developed, a child won't be able to reach out and grasp. If an organization cannot reconcile the confusion, or doesn't contain the requisite capabilities *or* adequately coordinate functions, it will not be able to perform reliably and consistently. Put simply, superior execution is very challenging.

Thus, even if the environment places demands on the organization and there is general agreement within the organization that a response is necessary, the organization may not be able to respond. The genius of the book *Execution* is that it articulates the dimensions and difficulties of execution and, most importantly, that execution entails much more than an automatic process of "just doing."[7] But for our purposes, we wish to emphasize that sound execution also involves *learning* and *improvisation*.

Very few companies operate as if the fire alarm just went off; instead, they manage to formulate and stick to some steady-state methods and procedures that at one time, at least, functioned efficiently. Successful adaptation, however, partly involves deviating from those states, or replacing them entirely. A company may have learned how to walk, but it must also learn how and when to run. Learning to walk may have taken years to master, but walking will do you no good when you are in the middle of the road and a car is fast approaching. In an excessively complacent culture, you'll never see the forces coming that can run you down. Execution presumes that basic abilities will develop and become increasingly complex in order to both extend the corporation's reach and recognize and react to new circumstances. The people of the organization must always be developing.

It never is a simple matter to gauge what an employee is capable of at any particular time, but we find the Soviet developmental psychologist Lev Vygotsky's concept of *scaffolding* to be a helpful guide when considering how to facilitate personal growth.[8] The idea is to identify the most advanced activity the employee is capable of performing with the assistance of others, assign that activity to the employee, and then ratchet up performance expectations to the next level of development. Clearly, growing the abilities of the workplace takes a lot of work.

General Steele of the U.S. Marine Corps reminds us that strict regimentation is required for preparation in battle. But once the battle begins, a certain degree of discretion is essential for success. That is, there is a template for action, but the soldiers must know when to deviate from a practiced routine given their situation. We think of the soldiers as being *fluent.* A fluent speaker, for example, has a rich vocabulary and knows the rules of grammar, but when delivering a specific message to a group, will depart from a script in interesting ways that incorporate events that preceded the talk and audience reactions during it. Soldiers, too, know when to depart from a script while remaining within the confines of certain rules of engagement and the dictates of their training.

Such well-chosen departures can be thought of as improvisations, as long as you don't associate improvisation with wild spontaneity. Successful improvisation requires a stable organizing structure, a right and wrong way of doing things, and a great deal of skill. In a jazz ensemble, *everyone* has to be a virtuoso and everyone must be willing to let others look (or sound) good.[9] That sums up what great leadership strives for: communities of excellence with members expertly playing off one another. This implies that meaning and actions frequently unfold over time, and the work of the leader isn't always to gain agreement among group members, but to foster coherent interactions even when ideas are not uniformly shared.

This brings us back to excellence and execution and a few requirements that organizations must nurture. First, novices learn how to play notes, but experts know how to play in between notes and how to improvise on a theme. Improvisation is evidence of facility within a discipline. Mozart thought the young Beethoven had promise when, during an audition, Beethoven proved he could improvise on the spot on any theme Mozart assigned—Mozart would have become Beethoven's teacher had it not been for Mozart's untimely death.[10] Unless the organizational culture promotes continuous learning and experimentation, people will only be able to perform in accordance with established protocols, note by note. Attempts to move outside of those protocols without the requisite fluency will likely prove disastrous.

Second, the act of improvising is a method of discovery. It can lead to novel productions. For example, in the Claude Renoir film *The Mystery of Picasso,* Picasso is shown experimenting and repainting his work. After five hours of time-lapse filming, Picasso announces he sees where he is going and, tossing aside spent ideas, begins with a new canvas.[11]

The bottom line: You have to learn to improvise, but you also have to improvise to learn. Both can be problems for organizations that "just want someone to do the job," but the latter usually is the more problematic, since it involves organizational tolerance of failure and the thick skin and self-discipline of a performer who must withstand scrutiny about what went wrong and make corrections accordingly. The drama of Picasso caught on film is how many paintings are discarded before getting to the one that is ready to be released to the public.

FIGHTING CYNICISM

This isn't a book on strategy, and we have offered these brief introductory remarks on strategy as context only. There are a host of books available that cover various strategic options, and you can go to these for specifics. Our purposes are to acquaint you with a basic framework into which most strategic actions will fall, along with a few basic executional necessities. With that behind us, we now are in position to explore what kind leaders can do to build adaptive organizations and favorably and wisely influence the strategic choices of their companies.

Many leaders have to combat organizational conditions that conspire against easy fixes and simple, ready-made solutions. They enter companies with histories, populated by employees who have had experiences with other leaders, many of whom have promised improvements and failed, and many of whom have offered new hope and have fallen conspicuously short. We used to think that the correctives leaders needed to make in order to produce thriving workplaces were a matter of righting past wrongs, demonstrating that one is a different kind of leader, and making operational adjustments with the intent of rekindling employees' enthusiasm for their work. The idea was to help employees forge new attachments to the organization and their jobs: That is, the perceived corrective was to cure disengagement.

But we now see that the pathology facing many companies runs much deeper than employees who are uncommitted and have emotionally removed themselves from the workplace. Rather, the pathological manifestation of maladaptation is cynicism. It is much worse than being disengaged and uncommitted. It is the attitude that all attempts at positive change and adaptation are doomed to failure and the most advantageous course is one of resignation: that the best one can do is tolerate one's circumstances as they exist. This is a sad state for individuals and for organizations, since the will to change has been lost.

Many years ago, the psychologist Martin Seligman and colleagues were experimenting with dogs in what is known as a Solomon Box.[12] The box has a partition in the middle, and the experimenter has the ability to deliver shocks to dogs on each side of the partition. When the onset of shocks is programmed to commence after a dog has been on one side of the box a certain amount of time, normal dogs quickly learn that by periodically traversing the partition and moving from side to side, they can completely avoid the shocks. However, dogs that were previously exposed to inescapable shocks (i.e., there was nothing they could do to avoid the shocks) did not act the way normal dogs do when placed in the Solomon Box. They remained on one side of the box and endured the shocks. If they happened to cross the partition, they failed to realize that they made an effective response. That is, they didn't learn.

You can imagine an employee asking, "Why bother?" "What's the use?" "What's the point of trying?" And they do ask. Viewed through the lens of maladaptive functioning, the organization is deprived of what people do best: think in a natural, healthy way. Instead, the organization is systematically impaired, and that intrudes upon, or disables, normal drives and activities. The result is a company that is competitively handicapped. It had better have a darn good product or service that most people want, because the company won't otherwise be able to withstand its own weight of lethargy and immobility, physical and mental.

We want to explore how the vitality of organizations is lost, as with the helpless dogs in Seligman's lab, and what makes vitality so difficult to recover. Or, conversely, what makes organizations vibrant, mindful, and alluring places to work? In either case, leaders are the culprit or the inspiration, respectively.

An ability to think straight is not a panacea for all possible organizational ills, nor does it assure success, but it does afford the best chance to take advantage of the company's collective intelligence—and there are such things as smart and dumb companies—and to make measured, effective responses accordingly. The best way to succeed, all else being equal, is for a leader to figure out how to get the best from everyone—and how to prevent employees from prematurely giving up.

Our basic prescription, discussed in the following section, is for the leader to produce a culture that has what researchers have called "absorptive capacity."[13] This refers to the ability of the company to extract relevant information from its various environments (e.g., regulatory, competitive) and transform those data points into usable knowledge. This chain of activities is necessary for generativity and adaptation, and some companies are better at its execution than others.

The effectiveness of a sponge depends on how much liquid it can absorb before becoming saturated. In organizations, this uptake is the first step in decision-making. The information must be distributed and worked upon, the implications of the data made manifest, and a determination made on what should be done with it, if anything.

This collective ability requires that people of the organization become progressively smarter so they know what new information they should gather, how it relates to other information on hand, and what the implications are. Otherwise, you end up with an organization that wrings out its sponge and soaks up the same stuff over and over again. What passes as "new" is merely recycled information about the same competitors, customers, and markets.

Then, of course, there is the "not-invented-here" syndrome, by which a company discounts anything outside of itself, essentially becoming an old, hardened, nonporous sponge. Consequently, it won't be able to redeploy resources where they are needed most.

This is a lesson that a resurgent Merck learned the hard way. By the late nineties, its research culture had grown exceedingly insular—refusing to acknowledge medicines discovered outside its labs or to readily engage in various mergers and alliances—and its pipeline for drugs was consequently drying up. It took a newcomer to the organization to revive the science within the company by convincing researchers that plenty of high-quality biomedical work gets done in other places and that Merck should actively seek access to that research. All indications are that the new openness has been a boon to Merck's financial status.[14]

As a process, absorptive capacity is like any other. If the company never develops a system of exploration, a means of fusing information, and an effective decision-making format, it will never develop a requisite capability for adaptation. Whatever the actual procedures and technologies a company implements in support of these processes, it will require people to actualize them. Thus, we now remark on the importance of culture in realizing organizational aims and the role of the leader.

CREATING POCKETS OF CULTURE

Imagine a large surface with pockets in it. The pockets vary in size and depth. Some are wide and deep, and others are shallow and narrow. If you were to drop marbles on the surface, most would likely roll into the widest, deepest pockets. And, if you subsequently shook the surface, the marbles inside the deepest pockets would have the greatest difficulty escaping, whereas marbles in the more shallow pockets would roll free and probably be captured by a pocket that has more accommodating space.

We liken a particular company's culture to the surface of the table with several pockets.[15] The pockets represent established, stable patterns of thinking, feeling, and acting. They represent what people actually do. The deeper, wider pockets are indicators of what people do more of, with greater intensity—and it's just the opposite for the smaller pockets. Culture sometimes appears to have an ephemeral and hypothetical quality, as if it is whatever executives say it is. Instead, culture is defined on the ground by the daily interactions of employees—by recurrent patterns of behaving.

The valleys of this topographical landscape, then, can be thought of as similar to attractors in physics—they pull behaviors from other potential states. The wider and deeper the pocket, the greater the pull. Although one could perhaps describe the entire surface in a few words, in truth, culture isn't monolithic. It may be dominated by a single pocket that over time has expanded to push out others, but usually there are a few different pockets, representing collections of people that interact in certain ways, scattered throughout the organization. Organizational development, then, may be conceived as the influences of behavioral sets or attractors that not only define current temperaments and activities but constrain future behaviors.

As a leader, you want the pockets in the cultural surface to support organizations that promote healthy employee interactions, guide employee aspirations and behavior, and can effectively adapt to changing conditions. In the following sections, we present opposing forces; in each, the former are advantageous to adaptation and the latter are symptomatic of cynicism. Our assertion is that kind leaders are far more adept at producing cultural landscapes that facilitate enterprise.

Our apologies for the following unabashed use of mnemonics to highlight the respective cultural craters we wish to encourage and discourage. But we find them helpful and offer them to you. The adaptive cultural set, O.R.E., stands for *openness, resilience,* and *engagement.* We stumbled on this acronym by pure chance. Our methods were guided by content, but we couldn't help ourselves from capitalizing. Ore is a material that is worth unearthing because its value far exceeds the costs of extraction. Thus, we think of O.R.E. as something worth digging up and processing.

The negative anchors collectively representing a cynical state and maladaptive functioning are represented by C.P.U., a reference to the familiar computer term. But we don't have the new, fast Intel chips in mind. We are thinking of older systems with outdated hardware components that are barely able to run newer software programs. The exasperated user feels like putting his foot through the monitor. So, for us, C.P.U. denotes poor performance, unreliability, frequent downtimes, and lack of functionality. We liken this organizational culture to an old, broken-down computer with a cadre of people who are *complacent, passive,* and *unimportant.*

OPENNESS VERSUS COMPLACENCY

Personality is composed of different constellations of traits that are generally agreed upon.[16] "Openness to experience" is one of those traits that endures from study to study, demonstrating its place as a key dimension of personality. Artists tend to score highly on this dimension, and given that we consider good leaders to be artists, it was no surprise that virtually every leader we spoke to described the value of openness with textbook precision.[17]

Open people tend to be imaginative, curious, independent thinkers who welcome novelty and variety and who are amenable to new ideas, approaches, and perspectives. In contrast, those people at the opposing pole of this trait dimension are more comfortable with the familiar and conventional. In organizations, these latter people are defenders of the status quo and tend to gravitate toward methods and solutions that rely on tried-and-true ways of doing things. Leaders who are open are seldom content with the ways things are and appreciate the potential for improvement and change. They are always on the lookout for how to make things better, even if everything seems to be working just fine the way it is.

Openness has been shown to be related to intelligence, principled moral reasoning, tolerance for diversity, aesthetic sensitivity, and creativity.[18] We will focus on creativity momentarily, but first a word on what openness is not correlated with: power, defined as a desire to control the social and material environment. It has been speculated that those who strive to dominate others reject new ideas that may impair their ability to control.[19] Furthermore, if parenting is again a worthy guide, it has been found that authoritarian and dogmatic parenting styles that emphasize conformity and rigid adherence to rules tend to produce close-minded children, and, conversely, open-minded adults recalled parents who were loving, warm, and supportive of their imaginative experiences and fostered relaxed, free-thinking environments.[20]

Most leaders will say that this is not a good time to undermine creativity in organizations, particularly in fickle industries like fashion or cool industries like technology. But every company needs to create and innovate in order to adapt and grow. It helps if the leader is disposed toward continuous improvement. Regardless, there are principles to keep in mind that can facilitate an organization that is willing to experiment and change.

Having a Prepared Mind

Robert Price's recently published book, *The Eye for Innovation* (Yale University Press, 2005), makes the central claim that "unless you are looking, you will never find it." Many people before Sir Isaac Newton watched apples falling from trees, but he was *looking* and observed what even those who were scientifically knowledgeable failed to notice. Serendipitous observations aren't made without curiosity.

Even when the social milieu is unreceptive to newfangled ideas, it's the desire to know—curiosity—that keeps inventive minds working. Curiosity energizes. For example, the works of Monet have been described as recurring, focused, and intense studies of the all-consuming problem of light. He investigated the properties of light in phases, using the materials of his trade: first, as light broke up on things (e.g., sails), then on how light broke up between things under different conditions and times of day (e.g., dusk), and finally on how light itself dispersed on reflective surfaces (e.g., water). Incessant curiosity kept him going.[21]

According to Eileen Fisher, one of the goals of a leader is to allow people to become consumed by an organizational problem or concern without venturing off on a tangent. In the words of Fisher, "We encourage creativity, but we put a fence around it." That fence consists of the motif for her clothing (e.g., simple, comfortable) and the materials and processes of the fashion business. But that fence has a long diameter, and there is considerable area to innovate within it.

We agree that stimulating both curiosity and a sense of adventure, when in the service of organizational objectives, is one of the most essential responsibilities of leadership. Ubiquitous inquisitiveness is a surefire means to foster personal growth, since creative people need creative others for sustenance. Refinements and breakthroughs are dependent on the transmission and interplay of ideas. This is best achieved when a leader establishes a climate for creativity, infuses the workplace with new challenges, and promotes an intellectually stimulating environment that encourages creative inputs from employees, engagement in professional societies, and collegial exchanges of ideas.

Additionally, leaders can endorse innovative projects by dedicating time and resources to them and by acknowledging their importance when discussing and evaluating goals. Leaders telegraph their willingness to entertain options and in so doing can support new developments or undermine them. Novel alternatives can be undermined by policies that are pro status quo and contra evolution, or more subtly disrupted by excessive red tape, intolerance for risk-taking and failure, and unrealistic constraints such as impossible time pressures—aspects of the organization that make any attempt to break free of tradition tedious and punishing. Whether the barriers to creativity are stated or unstated, creative people flee organizations that do not allow them to express themselves.

The End of Talent Management

The refrains of talent selection, talent development, and talent retention echo throughout corporate corridors. But our questions are these: "What kind of talent are we talking about?" "What do you mean when you say 'talent'?"

We think most people will hesitate to answer because we all assume we know what we mean when the topic of talent arises. Being "smart" doesn't help much, since most employable people are above average IQ. Being "able to do the job well" doesn't help much either, since that simply implies we are looking for experience and job proficiency, and all that requires is time. Indeed, "talent" searches often are euphemisms for "tenure" searches and decisions. And if by "talent" we mean natural virtuosity, it is not to be found in significant numbers. If raw talent exists, we wouldn't recognize it until it has already been cultivated.

The quest for talent is a lot like looking for the snark.[22] It is a search for a fiction. Exceptional achievements are more likely products of blends of attributes, including the substances of passion, discipline, and stamina. Our own treasure hunt, then, would begin with looking for the person who cares deeply about becoming the best and who has demonstrated a willingness to make the necessary sacrifices. But you won't find much of this in organizations that encourage uniformity above variability. The reason that continuous improvement is so difficult is that people persist at what has been successful in the past, which acculturates predictable, reliable solutions, not surprising or unique ones. The best leaders realize that to grow, they must insert the possibility of variation into the system.

Next, we would look for domain expertise—with a twist. If you do not have differentiated conceptions of roundness and squareness, try as you might, you will never be able to reliably put the round pegs in the round holes or the square pegs in the square holes. Thus, people with incomplete understanding of an area will be incapable of adjusting their ideation and behaviors to new realities and will try to force-fit pegs that no longer belong. But open leaders are are especially worldly and have diverse interests. And talent, which we assume entails both excellence and originality, requires precisely that sort of breadth. That is, the most talented people have a wealth of experiences to pull from. They are able to retrieve a wide assortment of information, examples, and concepts and sort and combine them in task-relevant ways. It isn't just the depth of knowledge that matters; the vastness of leaders' experiences, which yield rich conceptual structures, matters as well. We would think of these leaders as interesting people because they are interested people.

Jay Ireland's career and GE's approach exemplify the importance of cross-training—exposure to the broader domain of business and general management than the insular functional domains of finance, operations, and so forth.

Ireland began his career as an accountant and rose through the ranks, gaining exposure to various business units as he worked his way to the top of three different GE businesses: Plastics, NBC TV, and Asset Management. Expanded contact with different parts of an organization allows the leader to make inventive associations that would not be possible with a less nuanced corporate education. Combining familiar aspects of two different domains can stimulate novelty and invention. For example, try this thought experiment, which is a replication of one conducted by Kunda and associates.[23] First, describe the members of two respective categories: a Harvard graduate; a carpenter. Got them? Now describe a Harvard-educated carpenter. Two familiar concepts combine to create something entirely new.

Innovators and artists make these odd connections all the time *and* have the ability to see possibilities in them. Being interested, and curious, and adventuresome permits a person to find and recognize the potential in disparate ideas. For example, the central character in author Stephen Donaldson's double trilogy, *Thomas Covenant*, is a leper. The reason Donaldson knew Hansen's disease would work for his purposes was because he knew all about the disease and the habits of people who had it through the work of his missionary father. People with the disease have to be extremely cautious because they lose feeling at the tips of their extremities and are susceptible to injury and infection. It was just the sort of hypervigilance that he was looking for in his main character.[24]

Thus, if we were looking for "talent," we'd look for people who knew a lot about lots of different things.

Finding versus Solving Problems

Art has been described as the manifestation of the inchoate. It doesn't involve solving a nicely formulated, well-packaged problem that converges on one, and only one, solution, but rather discovering within the nebula of questions and ideas the problem that needs to be solved.[25]

It begins with the feeling that an organizational challenge begs for resolution; in turn, that vague sensation is reformatted as a problem.

The most important and inspiring problems don't present themselves ready-made, but are discovered by imaginative people who are able to see through the disorder of daily living and realize there is still much to be done. Masaki Suwa refers to this special visuospatial ability as "constructive perception." It is a self-disciplined, reflective process of attending in which individuals purposely look anew at something.[26]

Well-defined problems get most of the attention because those are the problems that can generally be resolved through analysis and standard operating procedures. It is much harder, and far more critical, to know which problems are the most important to pursue. We can envision each of our leaders turning facts around in their minds as if twisting and inspecting an object in their hands, thinking, "We are missing something. There is something else here—we just don't know what it is yet."

You want talent? Find someone who is willing to peer into the unknown and bring you problems.

Create Obstacles

Howard Gardner, the Harvard professor, recalls a time when he and others were discussing how to help make someone more creative.[27] Members of this illustrious circle of friends offered the usual advice: brainstorm, present interesting problems, and such. One member of the group, the philosopher Nelson Goodman, shook his head: "Create obstacles, and make sure they are productive ones."

We generally think of obstacles as something to be avoided: If encountered, obstacles will stop you in your tracks. Thus, we often avoid roadblocks and look for the paths of least resistance that allow us to keep doing what we do best or have handy in our bag of tricks.

But confronting obstacles head on, even hypothetical ones, does force you to reformulate your working assumptions and focus anew on the nature of the problem. Inventors who must constantly work against existing patents know too well that if they want to attain a particular outcome with the same functionality as other products, they need to figure out a way around or through the patent. This forces the question, "What would you do if . . . ?" This is a good question for companies to repeatedly ask, and as Nelson Goodman suggests, they may surprise themselves with the answers.

RESILIENCE VERSUS PASSIVITY

The second feature of our cultural terrain would be an ability to persist, self-renew, and flourish despite obstacles and uncertainties, without being incapacitated by hardship or the unknown. In various ways, our leaders described the psychological concepts of hardiness and resilience.[28] In general, these refer to the ability to keep one's wits about one and maintain positive functioning even though conditions may be trying. The leader remains competent in making use of personal and environmental resources in order to achieve her aims.

The sinkhole the leader is trying to avoid consists of withdrawal, passivity, and a feeling of injustice (i.e., being unfairly wronged by the vicissitudes of life). Basically, the leader is attempting to forestall a mental retreat. This can be a Florida-sized hole that swallows everything within its grasp . . . unless the leader takes precautions. A leader who blames and berates employees for their failings, while remaining personally beyond reproach, and who barks imperatives for improvement, while providing little support and direction, will not instill the steadfast resolve required for corporate success.

Organizational resilience, first, requires that leaders attenuate the negative effects of stressors. They primarily do this in three ways.

- *Provide a moral compass*: Life becomes so much easier when the solution to corporate dilemmas and adversity is simply doing the right thing and reminding oneself that, in the words of Chancellor Emeritus Dan Ritchie, "Some things just aren't for sale." It also becomes easier when actions are taken with a clear set of criteria and purposes in mind. Possible responses are narrowed to those that are consistent with corporate values and to what is personally important to the individual, usually involving the fulfillment of some larger mission through one's work. For better or worse, it is much easier to carry on when backed by the conviction that one did the right thing for the right reasons.

- *Encourage an active approach to problem-solving*: A critical aspect of coping is knowing that one is well equipped to handle whatever comes along: that one is well trained, that there are procedures in place to vet issues, and that one has the requisite resources and tools to gather information and probe for answers. That is, there are things you can do to meet challenges head on. As such, good leaders expend a great deal of time and resources on employee training, on process review and drill, and on problem-solving methodologies and procedures.

- *Create extensive support networks*: One of the most common characteristics of quality leaders is that they

discourage overreliance on themselves for answers to
all corporate ailments: "Don't rely on me, rely on one
another." They don't abandon their own role in providing encouragement and support, but emphasize that
the organization itself is a superb reservoir of helpful,
talented colleagues who gladly will lend a hand and
advice when needed and will ask for help when necessary. To facilitate exchange, leaders create cross-company
forums to discuss and debate issues and often introduce
formal mentoring programs to augment employee
growth, particularly early in an employee's career.
Knowing you have the willing, competent support of
others is an effective way to buffer the debilitating
effects of adversity.

In addition to these actions that essentially inoculate the workforce
against helplessness, there also are steps leaders take to help people feel
more in charge of their fates.

Embrace Change

Adaptation proceeds more peaceably if people perceive the challenges
associated with change as a part of the natural order and anticipate
and welcome change as an opportunity rather than an inconvenience.
This is not Pollyanna's optimism that celebrates misfortune, but a
more weathered variety with a rational basis. Most optimism is realistic, not the ambitious, solve-the-world's-problems variety. You
hope you will do well on an exam or will get a good parking spot or
will finish the project in time. You may be grandly hopeful for peace
on Earth, but for the most part, realistic optimism is tethered to the
here and now.[29]

The thing about reality, however, is that it is fuzzy, and one has the latitude to think the best or worst and still be well within the boundary of rational discourse. The difference between optimists and pessimists can be found within this boundary. Optimists do not berate themselves for what they could have done, and they approach the future with surety. Pessimists deny themselves little pleasures and, consequently, are not as psychologically prepared when events do not go as planned.

This, perhaps, is most dramatically evident in the way optimists and pessimists confront obstacles. Optimists use approach coping strategies, and pessimists use avoidance strategies.[30] Optimists attack the problem either by planning and seeking instrumental support from others, or by mentally making the event more palatable or manageable by the way they think about it. For example, a drizzly day could ruin a family reunion for some but not others, depending on how you think about it. A shower is not as good as sunshine, but it's much better than a downpour: How you choose to think about it can either ruin the day or save it. There is no denying it's raining, but it can be thought about in a more positive way. Pessimists will cancel the outing or make it a miserable event for everyone.[31]

Maintain a Sense of Control

There is perhaps no belief as central to personal well-being and performance as the belief that a person is an effective agent who has an impact on the events around him. That is, control involves knowing that one can influence outcomes and make a difference.

We suppose we could invoke the idea of empowerment as a proxy for control, but too often empowerment is misidentified as a *feeling* that one is a powerful actor. And feelings only go so far before the realization is made that either you can affect outcomes or you can't.

You either have control or you don't. Leaders understand that employees who believe they are capable of influencing change must have the latitude and discretion within their bailiwick to make decisions that will produce the desired results. A sense of mastery presumes that one has had the chance to be master.

This is much easier said than done because enabling others requires concern, patience, expertise, and tolerance. It requires the qualities and time that many managers simply don't have or refuse to give. Additionally, jobs are often so compartmentalized that incumbents don't see the effects they potentially have on others, nor do they receive the support and resources they might need to modify what they are doing to produce better end results. These aren't isolated cases: Too many people in companies feel disconnected from any meaningful outcomes and, as a consequence, seldom get to savor the thought that they are making a real contribution.

If leaders want employees who will pursue improvements and welcome challenge, they will devote the attention needed. Efficacy—or the belief that one can succeed—is an essential ingredient for organizational effectiveness.[32] Without evading the truth, leaders try to instill efficacious attitudes in the workplace and temper self-defeating ones. They do this by providing honest feedback and delegating authority. According to Dick Parsons, the best way to instill confidence in others is for the leader to treat them in a way that shows he has confidence in them. Delegation clearly signals a faith in another's abilities and an expectation of positive results.

The benefits are plentiful. People who feel capable tend to set challenging self-goals, volunteer for difficult assignments, put in the effort and mobilize resources to meet objectives, and persevere when confronted with obstacles. Less confident people are more prone to desert the goals when faced with negative feedback, social disapproval, or setbacks.

ENGAGEMENT VERSUS UNIMPORTANCE

Very early in her career, Roxanne Quimby said, she got her $199 worth from the one and only supervisory training program she ever attended. The lasting takeaway was this: MMFI, or Make Me Feel Important. We don't believe there is any worse feeling in *any* relationship than feeling expendable, that there is nothing so special about you that you can't be replaced. It is an awful feeling we don't wish on ourselves, the people who work for us, our children, or other people's children.

While researchers, consultants, and commentators spend a great deal of time advocating for a workplace in which employees are fully engaged, the consequences of failing are often more dire, organizationally and personally, than they may think. Feeling disconnected would be the least of worries. That implies the absence of any meaningful relationship. Although alienation can make for uncomfortable fellowship, people can usually get on just fine by creating an ample amount of psychic space between themselves and personifications of the organization, whether managers or co-workers. They simply do not involve themselves much in extra-role endeavors or become too concerned with the welfare of the organization as a whole.

Not caring or feeling any connection is bad enough, to be sure, but something else often happens in between the day an employee is hired and the day she packs it in. Employees feel *unappreciated*. The day a company hires someone, there must be at least some minimal hint of mutual attraction. The employee feels wanted, and the organization conveys it needs her. A good index of estrangement is just how quickly this presumption fails. Some companies begin their negative campaign from day one by forgetting it's a new employee's first day and being utterly unprepared for his arrival: no greeter, no office, no productivity tools. Nothing. Fortunately, new employees are willing to give their new employers the benefit of the doubt, and it usually takes another few months before employees realize they have entered a joyless, thankless place.

Conceptually, it isn't hard to know what people want within an organization. They want what everyone wants in any relationship of substance. If you ask yourself what makes any relationship satisfying, including intimate relationships, part of the answer will be to belong, to have pride in association, to know that your interests count, and to feel invigorated and alive. To continue this analogy of a close relationship, the idea is to create an *us with a future*.[33] We have discussed at length elsewhere how this is achieved in organizations, but here we lay out a brief four-point prescription.[34]

- *Belonging*: People are included in the decision-making process. They are informed of important organizational events, and their ideas to rectify problems are solicited, i.e., it matters what people think and can do.

- *Status*: The organization is successful on dimensions that are highly regarded by employees, to the point where employees actively tell others whom they work for. In order for an employer to transform many *"I"*s into a *"we,"* it has to offer something special that employees can grab hold of, i.e., the company has to be the best or first at something.

  Every organization needs to ask and answer these questions: Would it matter if our business closed its doors today? Who would care, and why? Is there anything about our company that makes us distinct and enables us to say that we make a genuine contribution to the world? Sam Palmisano used questions like these to rejuvenate IBM. Unless a company can offer something of special value that employees can grab hold of, it is hard to imagine that a vibrant, adhesive work environment would ever evolve.[35]

- *Trust*: Employees need to believe they are dealing with a reliable, dependable partner who espouses fairness and respect. We have discussed trust previously in the book, but the idea that we would incorporate here is that there has to be a sense of reciprocity to the relationship—that one side or the other isn't always taking, and giving too little in return.

- *Job Satisfaction*: People have to like what they do, and there are a host of ways in which work can be fulfilling—we need not enumerate the many, often discussed reasons here. We will summarize, however, by appealing to what we refer to as the three Ps of job satisfaction: people, process, and product. Basically, employees have to like and be stimulated by those around them (people), be continuously engaged with the physical and mental requirements of the work (process), and be excited by the meaning and contributions of work outputs (products).

Employees largely experience these things in their immediate work environments. The role of leadership is to convey the importance of these elements throughout the organization and assess managers on their ability to deliver upon the level of commitment for which the organization is looking. This will be harder in some organizations for certain types of jobs than others; it requires thought and effort. It requires . . . management.

Highly engaged adaptive cultures aren't the end-all to high performance, since there is more to motivation than this. One way to think about commitment is as fuel for a car. Commitment supplies the energy, but you also need a sound automobile with somewhere to go. That is, along with energy, there have to be ability and direction. Companies often mistake engagement, or intrinsic forces, for motivation, but it is very possible for a workforce to have lots of enthusiasm yet remain at rest for lack of the requisite capabilities and a well-defined destination. We are reminded of the comedy routine in which the football coach gives a stirring locker room speech and the enraptured team rushes toward the exits—to find the doors locked.

Although being satisfied at work does not in itself assure organizational success, a recent, and excellent, comprehensive review describes the many advantages of positive affect and happiness, which make vital contributions to success.[36]

- *Positive perceptions of self and others*: People who are happy are more self-assured and self-accepting and think more highly of others, considering them to have favorable traits.

- *Sociability and activity*: People who are happy are more affiliative, more socially lively, and more energetically engaged in group activities.

- *Likeability and cooperation*: Happy people are perceived as more competent, friendly, and approachable—the kinds of people with whom others want to interact and participate.

- *Prosocial behavior*: People who are happy show greater interest in helping others and are more courteous and charitable with their time and expertise.

- *Physical well-being*: People who are upbeat and positive report being healthier and fitter and are more involved in health-promoting behaviors and recreational activities (and, conversely, are less likely to engage in physically harmful behaviors such as eating poorly or smoking). Our wives encouraged us to ask our interviewee-leaders if they exercised. They do. Not only are the leaders with whom we spoke successful and happy, but they tend to be fit as well.

- *Creativity and coping*: People who are happy are more flexible and adaptive thinkers and more astute and mature problem-solvers. Unlike the image of depressed, brooding artists, in actuality, even those tormented souls had their best ideas when they were in good moods, as Mozart readily admits: "When I am, as it were, completely myself, entirely alone, and of good cheer—say, traveling in a carriage, or walking after a good meal, or during the night when I cannot sleep; it is on such occasions that my ideas flow best and most abundantly."[37]

Keeping commitment levels high in organizations has its advantages. We reiterate, however, that organizational performance involves not only creating a positive workplace, but harnessing that effect as well.

ADAPTATION REDUX

Innovative companies have a fundamental belief that there must be a better way. They manage to cut through convention and challenge pervasive assumptions about the way things are supposed to work. They are O.R.E. companies of great imagination, intellect, and resolve. Take, for example, the design of airports and the traditional setup at the ticket counter. We all know how airport check-in areas are supposed to look, despite the fact that few would say they are eager to reach check-in when traveling. The check-in process is a mess and one of the reasons passengers have to get to the airport early.

This is a perfect example of an assimilative strategy. The airlines have a particular operational view of the world, and for it to work as planned, the customers have to behave themselves, or else get shut out at the gate. Airlines could complement their approach with enrichment and hire jugglers and clowns to entertain while passengers snake their way to the front of the line. Or . . . the airline can conclude that there must be a way to alleviate travelers' stress.[38]

Airlines haven't been entirely idle, since they introduced self-help kiosks to speed up the process. But it was Alaska Air that changed the process by ridding itself of traditional ticket counters and by working with airports to reconfigure its areas. The results are promising, and other airlines are examining its patented process. We think this example is particularly instructive because it readily illustrates how companies can settle into proscribed procedures, and how difficult it is to break free. What's more, if we were to give groups a hypothetical design problem that mirrored the issues encountered in airports (we actually do a similar exercise and can attest to the results), no two solutions would look the same. That is, given the same materials, conditions, and constraints, every solution is unique. So why isn't every ticket counter different?

NOTES

1. deGeus, A. (1997). *The Living Company: Habits for Survival in a Turbulent Business Environment.* Cambridge, MA: Harvard University Press.

2. The concepts of adaptation offered here are a modestly expanded version of concepts famously introduced by developmental psychologist J. Piaget.

3. van Geert, P. (1998). A dynamic systems model of basic developmental mechanisms: Piaget, Vygotsky, and beyond. *Psychological Review*, 105: 634–677.

4. Lévi-Strauss, C. (1967). *The Savage Mind.* Chicago: University of Chicago Press.

5. Spencer, J.P., & Schöner, G. (2003). Bridging the representational gap in the dynamic systems approach to development. *Developmental Science*, 6: 392–412.

6. Kauffman, S. (1993). *The Origins of Order: Self-Organization and Selection in Evolution.* New York: Oxford University Press; Kauffman, S. (1995). *At Home in the Universe: The Search for Laws of Self-Organization and Complexity.* New York: Oxford University Press. Also see Lansing for a nice review: Lansing, S.J. (2003). Complex adaptive systems. *Annual Review of Anthropology*, 32: 183–204.

7. Bossidy, L., Charan, R., & Burck, C. (2002). *Execution: The Discipline of Getting Things Done.* New York: Crown.

8. van der Veer, R., & Valsiner, J. (1991). *Understanding Vygotsky: A Quest for Synthesis.* Oxford, England: Basil Blackwell; Wertsch, J.V. (1985). *Vygotsky and the Social Formation of the Mind.* Cambridge, MA: Harvard University Press.

9. Day, W. (2000). Knowing and instancing: Jazz improvisation and moral perfectionism. *Journal of Aesthetics and Art Criticism*, 58: 99–111.

10. Gould, C.S., & Keaton, K. (2000). The essential role of improvisation in musical performance. *Journal of Aesthetics and Art Criticism*, 58: 143–148.

11. Sawyer, R.K. (2000). Improvisation and the creative process: Dewey, Collingwood, and the aesthetics of spontaneity. *Journal of Aesthetics and Art Criticism*, 58: 149–161.

12. Seligman, M.E.P., & Maier, S.F. (1967). Failure to escape traumatic shock. *Journal of Comparative and Physiological Psychology*, 74: 1–9; Overmier, J.B., & Seligman, M.E.P. (1967). Effects of inescapable shock on subsequent escape and avoidance learning. *Journal of Comparative and Physiological Psychology*, 63: 23–33.

13. For discussions of absorptive capacity, see Cohen, W.M., & Levinthal, D.A. (1990). Absorptive capacity: A new perspective on learning and innovation. *Administrative Science Quarterly*, 35: 128–152; Lane, P.J., Koka, B.R., & Pathak, S. (2006). The reification of absorptive capacity: A critical review and rejuvenation of the construct. *Academy of Management Review*, 31: 833–863; Wang, C.L., & Ahmed, P.K. (2007). Dynamic capabilities: A review and research agenda. *International Journal of Management Reviews*, 9: 31–51; Zahra, S.A., & George, G. (2002). Absorptive capacity: A review, reconceptualization, and extension. *Academy of Management Review*, 27: 185–203.

14. Simmons, J. (2008). From scandal to stardom: How Merck healed itself. *Fortune*, February 18: 94–98.

15. Our idea of construing culture as a topography comes from dynamic systems theory. See, for example, Granic, I., & Patterson, G.R. (2006). Toward a comprehensive model of antisocial development: A dynamic systems approach. *Psychological Review*, 113: 101–131.

16. Ashton, M.C., & Lee, K. (2007). Empirical, theoretical, and practical advantage of the HEXACO model of personality structure. *Personality and Social Psychology Review*, 11: 150–166.

17. The following are representative articles on openness to experience: Dollinger, S.J., Ross, V.J., & Presto, L.A. (2002). Intellect and individuality. *Creative Research Journal*, 14: 213–226; George, J.M., & Zhou, J. (2001). When openness to experience and conscientiousness are related to creative behavior: An international approach.

Journal of Applied Psychology, 86: 513–524; McCrae, R.R. (1994). Openness to experience: Expanding the boundaries of factor V. *European Journal of Personality*, 8: 251–272; McCrae, R.R. (1996). Social consequences of experiential openness. *Psychological Bulletin*, 120: 323–337.

18. McCrae, R.R. (1994). Openness to experience: Expanding the boundaries of Factor V. *European Journal of Personality*, 8: 251–272.

19. Roccas, S., Sagiv, L., Schwartz, S.H., & Kafo, A. (2002). The big five personality factors and personal values. *Personality and Social Psychology Bulletin*, 28: 789–801.

20. See Dollinger, S.J., Leong, F.T.L., & Ulcini, S.K. (1996). On traits and values: With special reference to openness to experiences. *Journal of Research in Personality*, 30: 23–41; McCrae, R.R., & Costa, P.T., Jr. (1988). Recalled parent-child relations and adult personality. *Journal of Personality*, 56: 417–434.

21. Stokes, P.D. (2001). Variability, constraints, and creativity. *American Psychologist*, 56: 355–359.

22. The fictional animal in Lewis Carroll's *The Hunting of the Snark*.

23. Kunda, Z., Miller, D.T., & Claire, T. (1990). Combining social concepts: The role of causal reasoning. *Cognitive Science: A Multidisciplinary Journal*, 14: 551–577.

24. Ward, T.B. (2001). Creative cognition, conceptual combination, and the creative writing of Stephen R. Donaldson. *American Psychologist*, 56: 350–354.

25. For discussions of problem finding, see Getzels, J.W., & Csikszentmihalyi, M. (1976). *The Creative Vision: A Longitudinal Study of Problem Finding in Art*. New York: John Wiley & Sons; Runco, M.A. (2004). Creativity. *Annual Review of Psychology*, 55: 657–687.

26. Suwa, M. (2003). Constructive perception: Coordinating perception and conception toward acts of problem-finding in creative experience. *Japanese Psychological Research*, 45: 221–234.

27. Gardner, H. (2000). Project zero: Nelson Goodman's legacy in arts education. *Journal of Aesthetics and Art Criticism*, 58: 245–249.

28. For articles that examine the related concepts of hardiness and resilience, see Bonanno, G.A. (2004). Loss, trauma, and human resilience. *American Psychologist*, 59: 20–28; Maddi, S.R. (1999). The personality construct of hardiness, I: Effects on experiencing, coping, and strain. *Consulting Psychology Journal*, 51: 83–94; Maddi, S.R., Khoshaba, D.M., Harvey, R., Lu, J., & Persico, M. (2001). The personality construct of hardiness, II: Relationship with comprehensive tests of personality and psychopathology. *Journal of Research in Personality*, 36: 72–85; Maddi, S.R., Harvey, R.H., Khoshaba, D.M., Lu, J.L., Persico, M., & Brow, M. (2006). The personality construct of hardiness, III: Relationships with repression, innovativeness, authoritarianism, and performance. *Journal of Personality*, 74: 575–597.

29. Peterson, C. (2000). The future of optimism. *American Psychologist*, 55: 44–55.

30. Nes, L.S., & Segerstrom, S.C. (2006). Dispositional optimism and coping: A meta-analytic review. *Personality and Social Psychology Review*, 10: 235–251.

31. Schneider, S.L. (2001). In search of realist optimism. *American Psychologist*, 56: 250–263.

32. Bandura, A. (1997). *Self-Efficacy: The Exercise of Control*. New York: W.H. Freeman; Bandura, A. (2001). Social cognitive theory: An agentic perspective. *Annual Review of Psychology*, 52: 1–26.

33. Fincham, F.D., Stanley, S.M., & Beach, S.R.H. Transformative processes in marriage: An analysis of emerging trends. *Journal of Marriage and Family*, 69: 275–292.

34. O'Malley, M.N. (2000). *Creating Commitment: How to Attract and Retain Talented Employees by Building Relationships That Last*. New York: John Wiley & Sons.

35. Montgomery, C.A. (2008). Putting leadership back into strategy. *Harvard Business Review*, January: 54–60.

36. Lubinski, D., & Benbow, C.P. (2000). States of excellence. *American Psychologist*, 55: 137–150.

37. Vernon, P.E. (1970). *Creativity*. Middlesex, UK: Penguin Books, p. 50.

38. Carey, S. (2007). Case of the vanishing airport lines. *Wall Street Journal*, August 9: B1.

CHAPTER 6

PREPARING THE NEXT GENERATION OF LEADERS

A child and his father are hiking. They come upon a long suspension bridge that traverses a deep canyon. It gently swings in the wind that rushes through the canyon. The father looks at the boy. "We need to get to the other side." The father steps out first and walks a few paces before turning. "Come on, walk close to me." The child pauses. "Come on. We have to get to the other side, and I'm not going without you." The boy steps onto the bridge and quickly freezes as he feels it shake. The father explains that the bridge will sway a little, but their bodies will move quite naturally with it. They start up again. As they near the halfway point, the bridge's movement seems soothingly rhythmic and the wind warmly refreshing against their faces. The father stops at the midpoint: "Do you want to lead?" The child beams with pleasure. "Sure." And they continue to the other side.

Good leadership is like leading people across a high suspension bridge. First, followers have to feel secure enough to venture out, and they need to trust that the leader will be there if needed and will not let them down. Developmental theorists have referred to these as a "secure base" and "safe haven," respectively.[1] Second, they must convey that getting to the other side is a valuable endeavor, a worthy pursuit. Third, despite the fact that the trip may be treacherous, the leader must help followers to overcome their fears and to press on despite setbacks and unforeseen forces that urge them to turn back. Fourth, and perhaps most importantly, they must instill enjoyment of the journey so that followers will be willing to cross the bridge again and again, bringing along followers of their own.

The type of leader will determine whether and how people will cross our metaphorical bridge. Some, not trusting a gratuitous leader and believing the journey to be treacherous or meaningless, will refuse to go, but feign a willingness in order to honor the appearance of team spirit. Some will be pushed out and dragged across by the coercive leader. Some of them will fall en route; few will reach their goals with an attendant desire to repeat the crossing or the aptitude to get others to embark on the journey without similarly resorting to force. And still other leaders will coax followers across by successively dropping money in front of them: "You want it? Come and get it." "You want some more? Come and get it." Such leaders offer nothing but empty or unfriendly passage. Most importantly, they won't produce many people who are capable of getting out in front and confidently leading others.

Companies that are known for their superior management acumen exercise kind leadership. They offer exhilarating journeys that enable those who reach the other side to step off the bridge a different person. Isn't that really the goal and blessing of leadership: to help others along, to take pleasure in their achievements, and to watch as they assume progressively more responsible roles? And we want them to teach as they have been taught. In preparing the next generation of leaders, what is it that we will want them to know and be?

Try this thought experiment. If you were magically endowed with the power to produce in your children a limited set of personality traits, what would they be? There is a high probability that you would wish upon them those traits that would enable them to succeed whatever life circumstances they may encounter. Presented with a Rawlsian veil of ignorance—not knowing your children's destiny—the most prudent course is to equip them as best you can for as many contingencies as possible.

In a business setting, we would minimally want our charges to qualify as good business people by becoming technically proficient in their fields and facile with the myriad aspects of general management. There remains, however, the matter of becoming a good leader. To that end, of all that we have examined throughout this book, we believe that there are a few essential characteristics that not only foster leaders' own successes, but are critical in developing future leaders who share the same ideals and attributes. We realize that it is axiomatic to say that we recognize kind leaders because they produce people who have a character that is shaped by kindness. Yet it seems reasonable enough to surmise that mean dogs are produced by certain kinds of masters, and gentle, loving dogs are produced by other kinds. So what qualities do these leaders have and what types of people do kind leaders engender?

The four qualities that great leaders are able to instill in others are:

- Self-confidence

- Self-control

- Self-awareness

- Self-determination

How leaders achieve these ends and how these qualities manifest themselves in the workplace have been the primary rationales for this book. One of our conclusions has been that the way good leaders relate to employees compares to the way good parents relate to their children: setting limits, reinforcing autonomy and personal development, providing a positive example, offering a touchstone for moral truth and reality, and remaining open and sensitive to needs and concerns. What remains to be said is that the capacity to do these things well rests on the leader's ability to focus fully on others without being sidetracked by his own issues or unduly preoccupied with his own needs.

Before moving on, however, we revisit the analogy of the suspension bridge to summarize much of what we have discussed and to highlight the actions of kind leaders.

There are a few notable observations to make about leadership on our high suspension bridge. First, the follower is called upon to perform a daunting task. An ambitious, challenging goal is laid before him. In addition, the metric for success is unambiguous—to cross to the other side. There is no question about what must get done and who is responsible for doing it. The leader never really presents the task as optional, but conveys a firm expectation that this assignment is one that must be fulfilled. We can imagine the leader explaining why: that the follower is entrusted to deliver much needed goods to a customer or convey critical information en route to an important new discovery.

Second, the leader never negates the challenge by downplaying its magnitude. The bridge, in fact, is high and long. It won't be an easy trip. We are sure you can think of leaders who try to induce action by minimizing the risks: "It really isn't that treacherous (the rails will hold you in), and it really isn't that difficult (it just has the unsettled feel of a walk on a sandy beach)." The problem with this tactic is that it undermines the accomplishment; reaching the other side under the conditions described does not seem particularly momentous. Great achievements, by definition, are difficult to realize. Devaluing achievements by denying their worth is a spurious, shortsighted method of obtaining results.

Third, the journey entails transitions. The employee steps onto the bridge a neophyte, tentatively acclimating to conditions, and emerges on the other side a leader of the expedition. The follower's competence and confidence grows as she progresses to the point where she is able to function independently. None of this would have been possible if the leader wasn't willing to prepare the way and then step aside.

Expectations matter; the truth matters; growth matters. But none of this is straightforward, and getting people to take risks is seldom simple. That first big step is predicated on employees' trust in their leader and institution, and on the integrity of the underlying structure. Followers need to know that their weight will be sustained as they move forward. They will be all the more assured if the leader had previously prepared them for this moment through prior assignments and trials. Even so, although a leader may evaluate an employee as "ready," the employee may not be so sure (although most employees think they are more prepared than they really are). As a consequence, the leader may have to more forcefully prompt the employee to get moving, reiterating why the task is important and why the follower must proceed. And here comes the hard part. You, as the leader, may offer preliminary assistance and ongoing support and advice, but inevitably you must step back and watch what transpires. Most people will proceed without incident. Some will stumble and right themselves—or be gently lifted and set back on course. A few may fall and suffer both psychic and material damage, and you will have to hustle down into the canyon to resuscitate them and begin rehabilitation so that they can quickly regain their place and footing.

You may sense impending danger as the employee staggers across the bridge, periodically clinging for dear life. The one thing you can do is lend a hand. The two things you can't do are take away the project or send the employee back to the beginning. Once the assignment is made and the effort has begun, the outcomes now belong to the employee, succeed or fail. There are well-supported psychological reasons for this. For one, feelings of relief are rewarding, and by relieving people from tough situations, you reinforce giving up or turning back. People have to learn to work through the angst of peril and uncertainty. Second, by stripping employees of responsibility, you are clearly conveying that you have lost faith in your charge. It's one thing for someone who is insignificant in one's life to lose faith, but quite another for a leader or parent to lose faith in one. The latter is catastrophic, and some people never recover.

Expectations matter; the truth matters; growth matters. They matter because they make living a happy, gratifying life possible by providing in each of us the characterological wherewithal to achieve our own personal greatness. Appropriately charged by the leader, we are given the courage for fresh beginnings, the passion of purpose in our actions, the commitment to strive and to persevere despite encounters with our worst fears, and the reflective capacity to know when it is time to follow and time to lead. Great leaders give us the irreplaceable gifts of confidence, control, awareness, and determination.

FUTURE LEADERS

These four qualities—confidence, control, awareness, and determination—are not entirely independent. For example, leaders who are self-aware, who are attuned to their thoughts and feelings in the context in which they are generated, are better equipped to offer calm and measured responses—that is, to stay controlled. Those who are confident are better equipped to take personal responsibility for outcomes and to take necessary action accordingly, without prodding from others. Taken together, these qualities form a cluster of abilities that others may admire as aplomb and maturity.

Self-Confidence

Every year at the Oscars, we watch award-winners say that they owe their successes to one person or another. More often than not, these actors and actresses pay tribute to those people—including parents—who guided, supported, and believed in them as they pursued their dreams. We don't think of great stars as needing much help, and it is tempting to see their acceptance speeches as spectacles of false humility. Nevertheless, in truth, when they say they couldn't have done it without so-and-so, they probably couldn't have—at least, not as well. That is because the people they name gave them the irreplaceable gift of self-confidence: a firm belief in their capabilities and the expectation for success. Tom Renyi, chairman of the Bank of New York, claims it is the most valuable gift you can give to another.

Much of the recent work on so-called positive psychology rests on the observation that both pessimism and optimism are learned dispositions, and therefore teachable. People can either be paralyzed by self-doubt or be energized and enlivened by hopefulness and the conviction of one's capabilities. There is nothing more indispensable to one's personal welfare and effectiveness than knowing that one is the competent agent of what life has to offer: that we are the authors of our development, growth, and self-renewal. What impressed us most about the executives with whom we spoke was not only the degree to which they were prudently upbeat, but the extent to which their positive outlook and sense of mastery extended to events that most of us would regard as chance.

Successful executives naturally do not believe that they control the vicissitudes of life. What they can influence, however, is the way unpredictable occurrences are converted into meaningful experiences. It is only when the unsuspected is welcomed that it can be met with assuredness and the prospect of opportunity. Indeed, confidence in their abilities creates these situations in the first place. Those people who greet their worlds with confidence are much more adventuresome and have the personal resources (and resourcefulness) to meet new acquaintances, locate promising deals, and acquire interesting snippets of fact—even when stumbled upon by chance.

Hopefulness combined with self-confidence has other benefits as well. For example, it has been shown that people who are optimistic versus pessimistic are better able to see multiple aspects of a situation, think flexibly, anticipate future events and proactively take action, and astutely solve problems.[2] Despite these benefits, however, people will not persist at activities and struggle to overcome adversity unless they also think that their efforts will pay off. Thus, people who are self-confident must also believe they are competent, technically and socially, and able to succeed with the appropriate amount of effort. And good leaders are instrumental in perpetuating a healthy can-do belief system. This requires a special leadership skill to provide accurate performance feedback in a way that doesn't demoralize. For example, several of our interviewees let direct reports know that they can do better on particular assignments. Simple enough. But, the implicit message is this: Leaders convey to employees that they haven't done as well as they should have, but that they are perfectly capable of doing so. At once, they express faith in employees' potential and confidence in their abilities to live up to it.

Self-Control

A well-adjusted adult is able to control his impulses in order to maintain a healthy perspective on what is most important and advantageous to his welfare in the long run. A well-adjusted leader, who is presented daily with a host of distractions, must be able to cut through the clutter and avoid being derailed or consumed by temptations and ancillary issues. The proverbial low-hanging fruit that many managers reach for may be bad apples. Often these are diversions that use up precious time and resources and sidetrack leaders from the company's main focus. In essence, then, effective leadership requires the adult version of delayed gratification—the parallel of forgoing TV watching and other temptations in order to get good grades or become proficient in playing a musical instrument.[3] This means that everything the leader does is performed in the service of longer-term objectives, positioning the company to succeed over the long haul.

Self-control does not involve the repression of thoughts and emotions that arise from stressful encounters but, instead, the management of them, in order to maintain proper perspective on what is most important and to achieve longer term goals. Self-control has been likened to a muscle that can be overdeveloped and worn out with overuse.[4] That is, the more exertion required to maintain control, the more persistent the mental duress, the more compromised one becomes.

It is possible, then, to deplete psychic reserves—a condition that undermines future attempts at control and exposes leaders to hasty, poor decisions. Most of us have become mentally exhausted at one time or another and have noticed a marked decline in our abilities to tolerate additional pressures or that we become prone to ill-advised snap judgments. What's interesting about self-control is that when our resources are nearly depleted, we can often muster the resources to keep it together in one area (e.g., at work) but not in another; at home, we may become easily aggravated with the dog or eat too much. It's like plugging holes in a dam. Unless you find a way to relieve the pressure, blocking a leak in one place results in cracks and a leak elsewhere.

There are many little things that leaders do to help protégés master self-control. For example, Robert Price instructs employees to differentiate between "flea bites" and "alligator bites" and not to waste time and energy on the former by misconstruing them as the latter.

This is a helpful coping strategy that teaches future executives not to treat every new threat or problem with equal intensity. The value of this technique is that it moderates stress, manages anxiety, and allows one to remain in charge of one's faculties.

The most basic and essential means of fostering self-control is to establish goals that are worthy of pursuit. It is a blindingly obvious requirement that having strongly held long-term goals is a necessary condition for self-control. Otherwise, self-control is superfluous, since there would be no interests to subvert for the good of the future. But having aspirations is the easy part. Ensuring that the workplace sticks to the regimen by which goals are reached is the hard part, and our kind leaders have their approaches, as we have explored throughout this book.

We don't wish to be overly mystical, but we have observed in effective leaders a common aura that we view as two sides to the same coin. It isn't charisma: It's a healthy blend of insistence and concern that keeps people on track. One side of the coin is authoritative and particular: It says, "I'm serious; this must get done; don't mess with me." The other side is nurturing and facilitative: It says, "I wouldn't ask you to do this if I didn't think it was important and would be of great benefit to you—I'll give you whatever assistance you need to succeed." Giving orders about rigorous goals and standards is hard enough work for many a manager, but it's flipping to the other side of the coin that distinguishes the good ones. The followers of good leaders understand that the strongly phrased request is derivative of what the leader wants for them personally and professionally; consequently, followers are apt to accept the direction and diligently fulfill the request.

On the other hand, flip the coin of a marginal leader and you will read, implicitly or explicitly, things like: "Or else," "Hey, I don't make the rules," "It's not your job to understand 'why'; it's your job to do or die (metaphorically)." In this case, the follower provides grudging, half-hearted support while simultaneously expressing ersatz enthusiasm for the mission. It's the kind side of the coin that makes the difference.

Self-Awareness

Both of us serve as mentors to MBA students at a prestigious business school. During the first week of the semester, students complete a personality inventory and discuss the results in small groups. Invariably, intelligent people poke at the accuracy of the results in all sorts of creative ways. We have our suspicions as well about the reliability of many personality profiles. But the exercise is valuable because the habit of introspection is critical—not to the point of weighing oneself down with self-scrutiny, but as a way to reaffirm one's values and to notice one's effects on others.

Great leaders recognize self-awareness and personal examination as virtues because these keep leaders attuned to the kinds of people they wish to be. Conversely, leaders who become divorced from their moral centers are able to justify any act, no matter how reprehensible it may be. Leaders, including those we interviewed, will tell you that it is common for interests and values to collide within the marketplace, and that the most important orienting device when navigating through dilemmas is one's soul.

Periodically in this book, we have likened leaders to artists, and one area of intersection pertains to how leaders and artists choose to complete their works. For the good leader, this requires a great deal of introspection. Take the following example:[5]

The leader of a Himalayan expedition has the choice of either leading the final assault on the mountain himself, or staying behind at the last camp and giving another member of the party the opportunity; yet it is easy to suppose that no argument concerned with the interests of the parties will settle the question—for the interests may be precisely balanced. The questions that arise are likely to be concerned, not with the interests of the parties, but with ideals of what a man should *be*. Is it better to be the sort of man who, in face of great obstacles and dangers, gets to the top of the nth highest mountain in the world; or the sort of man who uses his position of authority to give a friend this opportunity instead of claiming it for himself? These questions are very like aesthetic ones. It is as if a man were regarding his own life and character as a work of art, and asking how it should best be completed.

The correct decision will be circumstantial, invariably involving insight into what the situation requires and how one wishes to be regarded by others. The important point is that without some degree of reflection and moral discernment, a leader won't consider the full range of options that are available to him, and—in this—will probably accept the default position of marching to the summit ahead of others, which is what leaders presumably do. Without self-awareness, the subtlety and nuance of leadership are lost, and the leader relinquishes the ability to formulate and convey the right message through his actions.

Peter Lorange, the former president of IMD (the global business school based in Switzerland), when reflecting upon the real-life case of the Norwegian explorer Roald Amundsen, notes that when Amundsen's team arrived at the South Pole, he insisted they all plant the flag together, using a moment of time to fill a lifetime with special meaning.[6] We wish some enterprising sorts would develop figurative ways of planting flags together in corporations. Years ago, O'Malley recommended a theoretical stock option plan that, like a piñata, would disperse options to all employees whenever the CEO whacked open the container by hitting his numbers. (By the way, Amundsen did not make it to the South Pole the first time he tried. But he learned from his mistakes, going so far as to learn the Inuit language in Greenland so he could gain insights into how the Inuit survived in a harsh environment, before returning to his quest.)

Self-Determination

By self-determination we mean that ownership of results resides with each individual. Responsibility for one's actions can't be carved up or displaced. It means there is always choice, and, yes, there are consequences for the choices we make. Producing a firm sense of personal accountability in others is one of the hardest tasks of leadership. It is difficult, first, because most people tend to see themselves as acting within a context of myriad influences—and there is a strong bias for attributing actions to a confluence of external factors: The time wasn't right, the resources weren't in place, others didn't do their jobs, etc.[7] Second, rather than hold people accountable, managers often let employees off the hook by rationalizing or avoiding employees' failings and thereby becoming duplicitous in excuse-making.

Kind leaders will have none of this. If you really want others to succeed, you have to fight your way through all of the obstacles that prevent honest feedback, and to combat the three tendencies people have to decouple, or excuse, personal responsibility from what has to get accomplished:

1. Denials of personal obligation ("It wasn't my problem")

2. Denials of personal control ("I couldn't help it")

3. Denials of clarity ("I wasn't sure what had to get done and what to do")[8]

There are many possible reasons why performance evaluations frequently lack candor: Managers are uncomfortable with confrontation; managers without a firm sense of what constitutes "excellence" accept lesser outcomes as "good enough"; managers didn't get involved in performance problems soon enough and agree that missed goals were unavoidable.

Of course, occasionally extenuating circumstances interfere, but true leaders are loath to accept excuses for missed deadlines, profit goals, or sales projections. The general sentiment is, "It's your responsibility. Let me know what you need, but a part of the success of this organization—and an important part at that—is finding a way around or through barriers in order to meet key objectives."

When a child comes home late because he "forgot his watch" or a company goes bankrupt because the CFO engaged in fraudulent behavior at the behest of others, neither crime is easily dismissed, and neither person's situation generates much sympathy. We expect people to be honorable—to keep promises and to safeguard their reputations—and good parents and good leaders hold them accountable for that. And, as unfortunate as it may be, there are consequences attached.

The goal isn't simply to reward or punish, however, but to convey the idea that people count on you, that there are standards to be met, and that it is up to you to live up to expectations, *no matter what*. We have heard that when plebes (first-year students) at West Point are asked a question by an upperclassman, only four replies are permitted: "Yes, Sir," "No, Sir," "Don't know, Sir," or "No excuse, Sir."[9] Truly, too many words and too much talking often get in the way of responsible action.

Our interviews with leaders may be characterized as much by what *wasn't* said as by what *was* said. None of them spoke about flat organizations, democracy, quality circles, and such. Indeed, none offered the pabulum of easy management and quick fixes. When they discussed execution, they talked about old-fashioned authority *and* accountability. They realize that accountability loses its stickiness when people are asked to satisfy organizational outcomes without having the requisite raw materials or decision-making power to achieve their ends. And they realize that authority without accountability results in possible abuse and waste. Instead, they instill bounded authority and accountability throughout the corporate hierarchy, as appropriate for each individual's level in the organization and preparedness to assume the responsibilities at hand.

Our leaders were emphatic that one good way to promote personal accountability is to allow choice. The way in which people internalize values and develop a sense of ownership in the care of the organization is through the habit of choice—and choosing wisely.

Most of what employees do daily is regulated only by their good sense and values. Michael Critelli of Pitney Bowes depicted the company's management philosophy as analogous to the way the company encourages good nutrition. At the extreme, it could eliminate bad foods from the cafeteria and serve only healthy pre-prepared lunches. It doesn't do this, of course. Instead, it proactively influences health by creating a social architecture that nudges people in desirable directions.[10] It charges less for healthy foods and more for unhealthy foods; it places unhealthy foods further away from the checkout counters; it promotes and nicely displays the healthy foods at the entranceway to the cafeteria; and so on. At no time does the company limit the choices people are able to make, understanding full well that character is built when there are options, some of which, if exercised, may be harmful to the people themselves and bad for the organization.

At the same time, successful companies know that people are fallible—precisely because they are people—and make it as easy as possible for them to thrive by creating environments that tend to elicit decisions that are in everyone's best interests. All behavior is regulated, intentionally or not. Why not create a culture and present options in such a way that people are more likely to choose what is good for themselves, others, and the organization?

We wish everyone in the workforce could experience kind leadership. Imagine working for someone who actually believes in you and wishes the best for you. Imagine being able to express an idea, challenge a convention, and work effortlessly and collaboratively with others. Imagine working for someone you trust. They're out there. If you want to find them, look in the faces of the people who are congregating on the far side of the canyon. If they are happy to be there, you know that you have come to the right place.

LEADERSHIP DROPOUTS

Final statements always are challenging. The one that we believe rightly provides a happy ending is, "People change." Rumor has it that we don't, but we do—and mostly for the better. Most of us have at one time or another resolved to improve some aspect of our lives and succeeded. And we are not only able to improve upon the superficial stuff, like personal appearance and habits of healthy living, but able to more fundamentally remake ourselves as well. We become more charitable, more proactive, more patient—and a host of other things that make us happier and more effective in interacting with others.

If you are one kind of leader, then, and wish to become another, there is nothing prohibiting you from making the change, which calls for hard work and a good dose of introspection. Insider accounts reveal that the head coach of the Super Bowl champion New York Giants, Dan Coughlin, had to shed his divisive old-school ways to survive a mutiny. He changed. He learned that gaining the cooperation of the team is far more advantageous than attempts to control the players. The results of Coughlin's personal metamorphosis were easily witnessed on the field, where the team played, well, as a team as opposed to a loose collection of individuals.[11]

If you don't consider yourself a leader at all, now is as opportune a time as any to consider why. After all, leadership is a form of expression, a way of communicating with others, as natural as banging materials together to make sounds or drawing on cave walls. Like art, it begs to be let out. From our perspective, not leading is unnatural.

The fact that many—too many—people dismiss their potential to lead has a couple of likely sources. On one hand, there is a tendency to associate leadership with organizational position, and, therefore, becoming a leader is frequently viewed as a logical impossibility, particularly by those who find themselves cast in nonmanagerial roles. On the other hand, some, fearing that there is one true way to manage, may be discouraged from trying, thinking that they do not have the requisite background that would enable them to get it just right. Thus, they relegate themselves to spectator status, believing that they are not up to the task. They become leadership dropouts.[12] On some occasions, they momentarily lower the white flag to become an odd sort of critic, evaluating others' leadership capabilities biased by their own low personal esteem. Thus, "Even I could do that" suggests that while the critic perceives the leader as worthless, the best she presumably could do would be similarly bad. Good leadership seems beyond their reach.

Perhaps leadership remains outside their grasp because what they really believe they can't do isn't leadership at all, but things associated with leadership that we sometimes reserve for a select few—such as notoriety and fame. But like the musician who toils in anonymity, the only requirements for leadership are a continuing passion for life's little pleasures, the effort to hone one's trade, and a desire to touch others in one's unique way. Leadership can be big or little and leaders large or small, but it is all grounded on the same native drive to create.

Kind leadership is available to anyone who wishes to be a part of any community. Stripped to its essence, its practice involves a mix of authoritativeness and concern, in equal parts. It is an interpersonal elixir that is warm but hard-hitting—like a good whiskey. And like that whiskey, leadership nuance and depth take time and care to perfect.

CONCLUSION

The workplace in America is changing, as highlighted in reports on television and in newspapers and magazines. Outwardly, life at the office is becoming less formal and constrained—friendlier, if you will—with open floor plans and casual attire, and a range of special benefits and allowances for employees, from flexible work hours to on-site yoga classes. These are the enviable, tangible trappings of companies that recognize a need to build cultures in which participation and inclusiveness are emphasized. This trend doesn't end on our side of the Atlantic or the Pacific. Successful companies overseas, particularly in Europe, are becoming more "consensus managed," and even Asia seems headed that way."[13] What exactly is driving these changes? Clearly, it's the emerging workforce—that all-important next generation of leaders: The population of young people that will be at the controls in the offices of tomorrow is not your grandfather's generation or even your father's, content to stay at one company for the long haul, performing a rote task or function. This upstart workforce, particularly the population born between 1980 and 1995, has much greater expectations and requirements.

Call them what you will—Generation Y, the Internet Generation, the Millennials—they have been coddled, protected, and hand-held from infancy into adulthood. In a fascinating *60 Minutes* report that aired in 2007, Morley Safer described a generation brimming with confidence and self-esteem, routinely rewarded and impervious to failure. They are also smart, resourceful, and civic-minded. At top business schools all over the world, students increasingly are interested not only in careers with "big bucks" but in doing work that benefits society.[14] Generation Y brings this ethic to the workplace where, as employees, its members expect to find a sense of purpose and connection, among many other qualities discussed in this book and engendered by kind leaders. Corporate leadership that is unable to meet those needs—not just by providing creature comforts but by instilling passion for one's work—will find itself on the losing end of the talent wars. In fact, not surprisingly, the most commonly cited cause of attrition for this generation of employee is that they don't like their boss or immediate supervisor.[15]

We admire Generation Y for its audacity and optimism. Its members are filled with potential and promise, and we have high hopes for them. They are why leading with kindness matters so much, now more than ever before. As illustrated in this book, some of the nation's most effective executives have built successful businesses on foundations of kindness and humanity. Kind leaders are well prepared for a trend that won't be bucked—a trend that represents the unmistakable look and feel of the truly modern workplace. A compassionate, appreciative, and forthright business environment is crucial in this era of workforce specialization, which places additional demands on management to secure the talent necessary to ensure that a company remains viable and competitive.

We began this conclusion by talking about a change in the workplace, but, of course, it's much bigger than that. American business is evolving from manufacturers of goods to providers of specialized, creative intelligence to a global market. It's a revolutionary change in the same way that the transformation from an agrarian society to a manufacturing economy was at the turn of the last century. To lead in this new reality, properly nurturing, motivating, and managing people is essential, or, rather, mandatory.

For the executives among us, leading and lighting the way in these exciting times, and to the fledgling talents about to take flight, a few final words—these from Albert Schweitzer—on preparing the next generation of leaders: "Example is not the main thing in influencing others, it is the only thing."

NOTES

1. Since Bowlby's seminal work (e.g., Bowlby, J. [1988]. *A Secure Base: Parent-Child Attachment and Healthy Human Development.* London: Routledge), several investigators have noted the parallels between leadership and the formation of relationships more generally: Davidovitz, R., Mikulincer, M., Shaver, P.R., Izsak, R., & Popper, M. (2007). Leaders as attachment figures: Leaders attachment orientations predict leadership-related mental representations and followers' performance and mental health. *Journal of Personality and Social Psychology*, 93: 632–650; Mayseless, O., & Popper, M. (2007). Reliance on leaders and social institutions: An attachment perspective. *Attachment & Human Develop-*

ment, 9: 73–93; Popper, M. (2004). Leadership as relationship. *Journal for the Theory of Social Behavior*, 34: 107–125; Popper, M., & Mayseless, O. (2003). Back to basics: Applying a parenting perspective to transformational leadership. *Leadership Quarterly*, 14: 41–65.

2. Carver, C.S., & Scheier, M.F. (1999). Optimism. In C.R. Snyder (ed.) *Coping: The Psychology of What Works*. New York: Oxford University Press; Snyder, C.R. (2002). Hope theory: Rainbows in the mind. *Psychological Inquiry*, 13: 249–275.

3. A good predictor of positive adaptation in life is an ability to forgo small, immediate pleasures in order to meet more important long-range goals. See: Metcalfe, J., & Mischel, W. (1999). A hot/cool-system analysis of delay of gratification: Dynamics of willpower. *Psychological Review*, 106: 3–19.

4. Baumeister, R.F., & Exline, J.J. (1999). Virtue, personality, and social relations: Self-control as the moral muscle. *Journal of Personality*, 67: 1165–1194.

5. Hare, R.M. (1965). *Freedom and Reason*. New York: Oxford University Press, p. 150.

6. Lorange, P. (2007). Explorer still offers lessons for business. *Financial Times*, October 22: 5.

7. Ross, L. (1977). The intuitive psychologist and his shortcomings: Distortions in the attribution process. In L. Berkowitz (ed.): *Advances in Experimental Social Psychology (Vol. 10)*. New York: Academic Press.

8. Schlenker, B.R., Britt, T.W., Pennington, J., Murphy, R., & Doherty, K. (1994). The triangle model of responsibility. *Psychological Review*, 101: 632–652; Schlenker, B.R., Pontari, B.A., & Christopher, A.N. (2001). Excuses and character: Personal and social implications of excuses. *Personality and Social Review*, 5: 15–32.

9. Gregerson, P.V., Sr. (2003). Integrity—Who needs it? *Vital Speeches of the Day*, 69: 270–273.

10. Since all behavior is motivated, the basic idea is to actively structure environments in order to encourage certain behaviors over

others. See Thaler, R.H., & Sunstein, C.R. (2008). *Nudge: Improving Decisions About Health, Wealth and Happiness.* New Haven, CT: Yale University Press.

11. Araton, H. (2008). A coach's about face transforms a team. *New York Times*, February 5: D1.

12. A parallel argument in the arts comes from Melchionne, K. (1998). Artistic dropouts. In C. Korsmeyer (ed.): *Aesthetics: The Big Questions*. Malden, MA: Blackwell Publishers.

13. Weber, E., Director IESE, NY, television interview, WLIW, New York, Oct. 26, 2007, with William Baker.

14. Horton, Ray, Columbia Business School, television interview, WLIW, New York, Oct. 17, 2007, with William Baker.

15. Sheehan, P. (2006). *Thriving and Surviving with Generation Y at Work*. Victoria, Australia: Hardie Grant Books.

John C. Bogle is founder of The Vanguard Group, Inc., and president of Vanguard's Bogle Financial Markets Research Center. He created Vanguard in 1974 and served as chairman and chief executive officer until 1996 and senior chairman until 2000. In 2004, *Time* magazine named Mr. Bogle as one of the world's 100 most powerful and influential people. Mr. Bogle is a bestselling author. More than 600,000 copies of his six books have been sold: *Bogle on Mutual Funds: New Perspectives for the Intelligent Investor* (1993); *Common Sense on Mutual Funds: New Imperatives for the Intelligent Investor* (1999); *John Bogle on Investing: The First 50 Years* (2000); *Character Counts: The Creation and Building of The Vanguard Group* (2002); *The Battle for the Soul of Capitalism* (2005); and *The Little Book of Common Sense Investing: The Only Way to Guarantee Your Fair Share of Stock Market Returns* (2007).

Michael Cherkasky is the former president and chief executive officer of Marsh & McLennan Companies (MMC). He served as chairman and chief executive officer of Marsh Inc., MMC's risk and insurance services subsidiary, from October 2004 until September 2005. Before its business combination with MMC in July 2004, Mr. Cherkasky was president and chief executive officer of Kroll Inc., the global risk consulting company. Mr. Cherkasky joined Kroll in 1994, rising to the position of president and chief executive officer in 2001. Prior to joining Kroll, Mr. Cherkasky spent 16 years in the criminal justice system, including serving as chief of the Investigations Division for the New York County District Attorney's Office.

Michael J. Critelli is the executive chairman of Pitney Bowes Inc., a $5.9 billion mail and document management solutions company. As executive chairman, Mr. Critelli leads the company's focus on the emerging opportunities in the external environment, including postal reform and transformation in the United States and globally, and market opportunities arising from the company's innovation and leadership in areas such as health care, government services, and corporate social responsibility. In his previous role as chairman and chief executive officer of Pitney Bowes, Mr. Critelli led the company through a period of unprecedented transformation and growth and firmly established its leadership in global mail and document markets. Under his leadership as CEO, the company was transformed from a collection of diverse businesses into a focused Mailstream industry leader, while increasing revenue by 50 percent.

Jesse Fink is co-founder and managing director of MissionPoint Capital Partners, a private investment firm focused on financing and accelerating the transition to a low-carbon and sustainable economy. Mr. Fink co-founded priceline.com and served as its founding COO from inception through IPO. In 1999, he formed his family office, Marshall Street Management. His philanthropic activities are synergistic with the MissionPoint platform and are executed through the Betsy and Jesse Fink Foundation, which invests in catalytic initiatives through environmental NGOs and educational institutions. He also serves on Environmental Defense's National Council and the Advisory Board of the Yale Center for Environmental Law and Policy.

Eileen Fisher is the chief executive officer of Eileen Fisher Clothing, which was founded in 1984 on a vision of versatile clothing that supports women's lives. The collection is sold by major retailers and specialty stores across the United States and Canada, as well as in 39 company-owned stores. Originally from Illinois, Fisher moved to New York City in 1973 to work first as an interior designer, then as a graphic artist. In 1984, she began her clothing business with $350, based on her idea of providing women with simple, high-quality, comfortable clothes that they could assemble as a "clothing system." She designed two tops, a pair of cropped pants, and a V-neck vest; cut the fabric on her apartment floor; and carried it by subway to a seamstress in Queens. No tassels, no underwire, no florals, and no nonsense. After one trade show, eight stores ordered them. Her company's clothes are now sold at sophisticated shops across the country, and her company is routinely described as one of the best places to work.

Rick Goings is chairman and chief executive officer of Tupperware Brands Corporation. Tupperware Brands Corporation is a global direct seller of premium, innovative products across multiple brands and categories through an independent sales force of approximately 1.9 million. Product brands and categories include food preparation, storage and serving solutions for the kitchen and home through the Tupperware brand, and beauty and personal care products through its Avroy Shlain, BeautiControl, Fuller, NaturCare, Nutrimetics, Nuvo, and Swissgarde brands. Following college, Goings founded one of the nation's first direct sellers of home security systems. He then held a number of senior management positions at Avon Products, Inc. in Europe and Asia, ultimately serving as president of Avon USA. He joined the Sara Lee Corporation in the early 1990s as corporate senior vice president in charge of household products and president of Sara Lee Global Direct Selling.

Jay Ireland is president and CEO of GE Asset Management, a position he assumed in June 2007. In this role, Mr. Ireland oversees an organization responsible for the management of more than 200 institutional accounts and approximately $196 billion in assets as of December 31, 2006. He also oversees the firm's management, distribution, and servicing efforts for an array of mutual funds. Mr. Ireland is a GE officer and a member of the Corporate Executive Council and the GE Capital Board of Directors. Prior to GE Asset Management, Mr. Ireland was president of NBC Universal Television Stations and Network Operations since December 2006. In this role, he had overall executive responsibility for NBC Universal's ten television stations, the Telemundo network and its sixteen Spanish language television stations, domestic first-run syndication, affiliate relations, and network operations. Before joining NBC, Mr. Ireland was CFO of GE Plastics since 1997.

Robert W. Lane has served as chairman and chief executive officer of Deere & Company since August 2000. Lane, following an early career in global banking, joined John Deere in 1982, initially managing various operations within the Worldwide Construction Equipment Division and later serving as president and chief operating officer of Deere Credit, Inc. In 1992, he joined the Worldwide Agricultural Equipment Division, where, as senior vice president, he directed equipment operations in Latin America, Australia, and East Asia. Elected chief financial officer in 1996, Lane subsequently moved to Germany, where as managing director, he led Deere's agricultural equipment operations in Europe, Africa, the Middle East, India, and the nations of the former Soviet Union. He returned to the United States as president of the Worldwide Agricultural Equipment Division and thereupon was elected president and chief operating officer of Deere & Company. Lane also serves as a director of General Electric Company and Verizon Communications, Inc.

Richard C. Levin is the longest serving Ivy League president and is recognized as one of the leaders of American higher education. A distinguished economist, he has served as chair of Yale's Economics Department and has been a member of Yale's faculty since 1974. The internationalization of Yale has been one of President Levin's priorities during his leadership. During his tenure, he launched the Yale Center for the Study of Globalization, headed by former president of Mexico Ernesto Zedillo, and created the Yale World Fellows Program, which is building and training a worldwide network of emerging leaders. Under President Levin's leadership, Yale completed a $1.7 billion fund-raising campaign and invested more than $2 billion in campus renovation and building programs. To ensure Yale's preeminence in research and discovery, he has committed $1 billion to renovating and expanding Yale's medical and science facilities, including the construction of five new science and engineering buildings; one of the largest new medical research facilities in the United States has recently opened.

Richard D. Parsons is chairman of the board of Time Warner, whose businesses include filmed entertainment, interactive services, television networks, cable systems, and publishing. From May 2002 to December 2007, Mr. Parsons served as Time Warner's chief executive officer. He became chairman of the board in May 2003. As CEO, Mr. Parsons led Time Warner's turnaround and set the company on a solid path toward achieving sustainable growth. In the process, he put in place the industry's most experienced and successful management team, strengthened the company's balance sheet and simplified its corporate structure, and carried out a disciplined approach to realigning the company's portfolio of assets to improve returns. In its January 2005 report on America's Best CEOs, *Institutional Investor* magazine named Mr. Parsons the top CEO in the entertainment industry.

John E. Pepper, Jr., is chairman of the board of the Walt Disney Company and serves as co-chair of the board of the National Underground Railroad Freedom Center. He served as vice president of finance and administration at Yale University from January 2004 to December 2005. Prior to that, he served as chairman of the executive committee of the board of directors of the Procter & Gamble Company until December 2003. Since 1963, he has served in various positions at Procter & Gamble, including chairman of the board from 2000 to 2002, chief executive officer and chairman from 1995 to 1999, president from 1986 to 1995, and director from 1984 to 2003. Mr. Pepper serves on the board of Boston Scientific Corp. and is a member of the executive committee of the Cincinnati Youth Collaborative.

Peter G. Peterson is chairman of the Blackstone Group, a private investment banking firm he co-founded in 1985. He is chairman of the Council on Foreign Relations and founding chairman of the Institute for International Economics (Washington, DC). Mr. Peterson is also co-chair of the Conference Board's Commission on Public Trust and Private Enterprise, along with John Snow, former U.S. secretary of the treasury. Mr. Peterson was chairman and CEO of Lehman Brothers (1973–1977), and after the merger with Kuhn, Loeb, became chairman and CEO of Lehman Brothers Kuhn Loeb Inc. (1977–1984). During his term, Mr. Peterson led the firm from significant operating losses to five consecutive years of record profits, with a return on equity among the highest in the investment banking industry. He is a former secretary of commerce under President Nixon.

Joseph Polisi is the president of the Juilliard School. Before coming to Juilliard, Dr. Polisi was dean of the University of Cincinnati College-Conservatory of Music (1983–1984), dean of faculty at the Manhattan School of Music (1980–1983), and executive officer of the Yale University School of Music (1976–1980). He became the sixth president of the Juilliard School in September 1984, bringing to that position his previous experience as a college administrator; a writer in the fields of music, public policy, and the arts; and an accomplished bassoonist. He was instrumental in the construction of the Juilliard Residence Hall and has focused his tenure on "community building." He is the author of *The Artist as Citizen*, a book that implores the classical music world to reach out to society at large.

Robert M. Price is president and CEO of PSV, Inc. PSV offers services in technology commercialization, corporate strategy, human resource management, and general management practice. Formerly, Mr. Price was the chairman of the board and chief executive officer of Control Data Corporation (now Ceridian Corporation), succeeding the company's founder, William C. Norris. Price joined Control Data in 1961 as a mathematician staff specialist and became director, International Operations, in 1963; group vice president, Services, in 1972; and president and chief operating officer in 1980. Price was instrumental in leading Control Data's early strategic expansion into international arenas, as well as its strategic move from hardware into information and systems integration services. In May of 1996, Price was elected chairman and CEO of International Multifoods Corporation, following the resignation of its then chief executive officer. Price helped guide the strategic repositioning of the company while successfully concluding the search for a new chief executive officer in January of 1997.

Roxanne Quimby is the former chief executive officer of Burt's Bees. As far as success stories go, Roxanne Quimby, the entrepreneur behind the wildly successful Burt's Bees, is one for the books. Quimby was a divorced mother of twin girls, living without electricity on a farm in central Maine, when she met local beekeeper Burt Shavitz in 1984. Shavitz was selling honey at a roadside stand. Soon the pair became partners. Quimby retooled Shavitz's wares, putting the honey in beehive-shaped designs with handmade labels and selling them at craft fairs. Not long after, Quimby also began selling handcrafted beeswax candles that she made in her kitchen. Burt's Bees continued to grow, and Quimby eventually created a line of 150 natural skin and body products, driving the company's sales to $50 million.

Tom Renyi is executive chairman of the Bank of New York Mellon, where he oversees the global integration of the people, technology, and capabilities of the predecessor companies, the Bank of New

York Company, Inc. and Mellon Financial Corporation. Prior to the July 2007 merger, Mr. Renyi served as chairman and chief executive officer for the Bank of New York Company, Inc., successfully directing that company's transformation from a traditional commercial bank to a global leader in securities servicing for issuers, investors, and financial intermediaries. After becoming chief executive officer in 1997, he accelerated the Bank of New York's strategic evolution through more than 80 acquisitions.

Daniel L. Ritchie is the chairman and chief executive officer of the Denver Center for the Performing Arts, one of the largest cultural complexes in the United States of America. From 2005 to 2007 he was chairman of the board of the University of Denver, where he had served as the sixteenth chancellor for sixteen years from 1989 to 2005. He was chairman and chief executive officer of Westinghouse Broadcasting for eight years before moving to Colorado in 1987. He currently chairs the education committee of the National Park System Advisory Board and is president of the Temple Hoyne Buell Foundation, whose focus is early childhood education and development. In 1998, the National Western Stock Show Association named Ritchie its "Citizen of the West." The award, one of his many honors, exemplifies the spirit and determination of the western pioneer. Ritchie holds both undergraduate and MBA degrees from Harvard.

Maria Rodale is the chairman of the board of Rodale Inc., the world's leading publisher of information on healthy, active lifestyles. Since joining the board in 1991, serving as vice chairman since 1999, she has helped build an international multimedia company from the small publishing business started by her late grandfather. In 1998, she served as director of strategy, where she led the strategic review, planning processes, and management changes that refocused the company on publishing information on healthy, active lifestyles. Ms. Rodale is the author of four books: *It's My Pleasure*, co-written with her daughter, Maya Rodale (publication date, May 2005, published by the Free

Press), and, published by Rodale, *Maria Rodale's Organic Gardening* (1998), *Maria Rodale's Organic Gardening Companion* (1999), and *Betty's Book of Laundry Secrets* (2001).

Robert E. Rubin is a director and chairman of the Executive Committee of Citi and has been involved with financial markets and our nation's public policy debates all of his professional life. Mr. Rubin began his career in finance at Goldman, Sachs & Company in New York City in 1966. He served as vice chairman and co-chief operating officer from 1987 to 1990 and as co-senior partner and co-chairman from 1990 to 1992. From 1995 to 1999, Mr. Rubin served as the seventieth U.S. secretary of the treasury. As secretary of the treasury, Mr. Rubin played a leading role in many of the nation's most important policy debates. He was involved in balancing the federal budget; opening trade policy to further globalization; acting to stem financial crises in Mexico, Asia, and Russia; helping to resolve the impasse between Congress and the executive branch over the public debt limit; safeguarding the nation's currency against counterfeiting; and guiding sensible reforms at the Internal Revenue Service.

Richard K. Smucker is president and co-CEO of the J.M. Smucker Company, makers of the leading U.S. brand of jams, jellies, and preserves. Smucker also owns Jif, the number-one peanut butter brand, as well as Crisco—all three are American icon brands. In addition, it produces extensive lines of ice cream toppings, natural peanut butter, juices, and other food products. He is the great-grandson of J. M. (Jerome Monroe) Smucker, who founded the company bearing his name in Orrville, Ohio, in 1897.

General Martin Steele is a retired three-star general and one of the most decorated officers in the Marine Corps, earning a rank of lieutenant general. After serving in Operation Desert Shield/Desert Storm, General Steele took over as director of the Warfighting Development Integration Division at Quantico. In 1993, he was promoted to brigadier general and assigned duty as commanding general, Marine Corps Base, Quantico, in June of that year. He was selected in November 1994 for promotion to major general. He served as the director of Strategic Planning and Policy, U.S. Forces Pacific, from 1995 to 1997. He was then promoted to lieutenant general and assigned as Deputy Chief of Staff for Plans, Policies, and Operations at HQMC. Upon retirement in 1999, General Steele became president and CEO of the Intrepid Sea, Air & Space Museum in New York City, the largest naval museum in the world. Currently, he is a managing partner of Uncommon Leadership, LLC, a leadership consulting company whose mission is to develop uncommon leaders of character across a wide audience range, including transitioning Marines, college students, and administrators, as well as corporate-level executives.

Andy Stern is the president of the 1.9-million-member Service Employees International Union (SEIU), the fastest-growing union in North America. Called "a different kind of labor chief" and a "courageous, visionary leader who charted a bold new course for American unionism," Stern began working as a social service worker and member of SEIU Local 668 in 1973 and rose through the ranks before his election as SEIU president in 1996. Stern is the author of the book *A Country That Works* (Free Press), which offers a fresh prescription for the vital political and economic reforms America needs to get back on track.

Josh Weston is former chairman, CEO, and chief operating officer of Automatic Data Processing (ADP). Mr. Weston headed an international service company of 30,000 employees that aids the management of industrial, retail, nonprofit, financial, and government organizations, bringing in $5 billion in revenues. Weston led ADP, the largest payroll and tax filing processor in the world, through 164 consecutive quarters of double-digit growth. He joined ADP in 1970, served as CEO from 1982 to 1996, and retired as chairman in 1998.

Bob Wright is vice chairman of the board and executive officer of General Electric Company and former CEO of NBC Universal, Inc. He joined GE in 1969 as a staff lawyer, leaving in 1970 for a judicial clerkship. He rejoined GE in 1973 as a lawyer for GE Plastics, subsequently serving in several leadership positions with that business. In 1980, he became president of Cox Cable Communications and rejoined GE in 1983 as vice president of the housewares and audio businesses. In 1984, he became president and chief executive officer of General Electric Financial Services and, in 1986, was elected president and chief executive officer of National Broadcasting Company, Inc. In 2000, he was elected chairman and chief executive officer of NBC and vice chairman of the board and executive officer of GE. He was the chairman and CEO of NBC Universal, Inc., from 2004 to 2007.